SECOND EDITION

Student's Book

3

SUPER MINDS

Herbert Puchta · Peter Lewis-Jones · Günter Gerngross

CAMBRIDGE
UNIVERSITY PRESS

Map of the book

Meet The Explorers (pages 4–9)

Vocabulary	Language focus	Story
Revision of numbers	• *Be good at* + *ing* • Possessive apostrophe	**Story** *The old book* **Value** Courage **Phonics** Short vowel sounds

▶ Song: The Explorers

1 Our school (pages 10–21)

What kinds of puzzles are there?

Vocabulary	Language focus	Story	Skills	Think and learn
School subjects	• *Like / Don't like* + *ing* • *Have to* + infinitive	*Getting help* **Phonics** Letter names	• Reading • Reading, listening and speaking **Value** Accepting others	Maths: Geometrical shapes

▶ Song: Lots of puzzles ▶ Communication: Favourite subjects ▶ Writing: My portfolio

2 The picnic (pages 22–33)

What's good to eat?

Vocabulary	Language focus	Story	Skills	Think and learn
Food	• Questions and answers with *some* and *any* • Suggestions	*The golden apple* **Value** Perseverance **Phonics** The sounds /ɪ/ and /aɪ/	• Listening, reading and speaking • Reading and writing	Science: Edible plants

▶ Song: Good idea ▶ Communication: At the sandwich shop ▶ Writing: My favourite foods

3 Daily tasks (pages 34–45)

What's it like to work at night?

Vocabulary	Language focus	Story	Skills	Think and learn
Daily tasks	• Telling the time • Adverbs for time	*Tidying up* **Phonics** The letter sounds *v* and *f*	• Reading • Writing, listening and speaking **Value** Being kind to others	Social science: Jobs at night

▶ Song: Night time flight ▶ Communication: Helping at home ▶ Writing: My family

4 Around town (pages 46–57)

What do we find in towns?

Vocabulary	Language focus	Story	Skills	Think and learn
Towns	• Prepositions • *Be going to* + infinitive of purpose	*Up high* **Value** Lateral thinking **Phonics** The sounds /aː/ and /r/	• Reading • Listening, speaking and writing	Geography: Tall buildings

▶ Song: Lost in town ▶ Communication: Help a visitor in your town ▶ Writing: Messages

5 Under the sea (pages 58–69)

What's in the sea?

Vocabulary	Language focus	Story	Skills	Think and learn
Sea creatures	• *Was* / *Were* • Questions and answers with *was* / *were*	**Story** *The trap* **Phonics** The letter sounds *s* and *sh*	• Reading • Writing, listening and speaking **Value** Being brave	Environmental studies: People and the sea

▶ Song: The Crocorox ▶ Communication: Where were we ... ? ▶ Writing: Sea creatures

6 Gadgets (pages 70–81)

How are gadgets useful?

Vocabulary	Language focus	Story	Skills	Think and learn
Technology	• Comparatives • Superlatives	**Story** *The cave* **Value** Being resourceful **Phonics** Long vowel sounds	• Reading and speaking • Listening, speaking and writing	History: Cave paintings

▶ Song: Look at my gadget ▶ Communication: Go shopping ▶ Writing: My gadgets

7 In the hospital (pages 82–93)

What keeps us healthy?

Vocabulary	Language focus	Story	Skills	Think and learn
Health	• Past simple: regular verbs • Past simple: irregular verbs	**Story** *At the hospital* **Phonics** *–ed* endings	• Reading • Reading and listening **Value** Determination, never giving up	Science: Keeping healthy

▶ Song: An apple a day ▶ Communication: At the doctor's ▶ Writing: Write a story

8 Around the world (pages 94–105)

What wonders of the world are there?

Vocabulary	Language focus	Story	Skills	Think and learn
Countries	• Negatives with past simple • Questions and answers with past simple	**Story** *The final letters* **Value** Showing interest in other cultures **Phonics** The sounds /iː/ and /ɪ/	• Listening and reading • Speaking, reading and writing	Geography: Wonders of the world

▶ Song: All the wonders in the world ▶ Communication: What did we do on our holidays? ▶ Writing: Write about a country

9 Holiday plans (pages 106–117)

How are holidays different?

Vocabulary	Language focus	Story	Skills	Think and learn
Weather	• Future with *be going to* + infinitive • Questions and answers with *be going to* + infinitive	**Story** *The treasure* **Phonics** The sound /ɜː/	• Reading • Reading and listening **Value** Changing perceptions	History: Holidays in the past

▶ Song: Happy holiday ▶ Communication: Holiday time ▶ Writing: Imagine a holiday

• **Language focus:** pages 118–128

Practice of creative thinking, critical thinking and cognitive skills.

Meet The Explorers

Meet Ben and Lucy – The Explorers. These two friends and their dog, Buster, find lost treasure and give it to museums. Their lives are very exciting. Today they are starting a new adventure. They are in a castle. They are looking for an old book. The book tells the secret of some lost treasure. But they are not the only people looking for the book …

1 001 **Listen and say the words. Then check with a friend.**

1 upstairs
2 twenty-one – fifty
3 downstairs
4 fifty-one – one hundred
5 cellar

2 002 **Listen and answer.**

1 What do Ben and Lucy want to find?
2 Where are they?
3 Where does Lucy want to go?
4 Where is the cellar?

3 **Close your book. Play the memory game.**

Where's … ?

Upstairs.

1 Look, read and write *B* (Ben) or *L* (Lucy).

1 Who am I? I'm not good at flying a kite. B
2 I'm good at riding bikes. Am I Ben or Lucy? ______
3 I'm not good at playing the guitar. Who am I? ______
4 I'm very good at snorkelling. Can you guess my name? ______
5 I'm good at climbing trees. What's my name? ______
6 Who am I? I'm really good at doing puzzles. ______

2 Put the words in order. Say the sentences.

1 good football. I'm playing at
2 I guitar. playing not good at the 'm

3 Watch, listen and say.

003

Language focus

I'**m good at** climb**ing** trees. I'**m good at** play**ing** football. Oops!
I'**m good at** catch**ing** flies. I'**m not good at** tell**ing** lies!

4 Look and make sentences.

	×	✓	✓
	✓	✓	×

Lucy isn't good at painting.

1 004 Listen and say what Ben and Lucy are good at. Then sing the song.

The Explorers.
Here they come.
Lucy and Ben.
Adventure and fun.

The Explorers.
Here they are.
Ben and Lucy.
Action stars.

She's good at doing puzzles,
She always finds the clues,
And reads them very carefully,
They tell her what to do.

The Explorers ...

He's good at riding horses,
And swimming in the sea.
He's an action hero,
Just like you and me.

The Explorers ...

2 Ask and answer.

3 What are you good at? Write a verse.

I'm good at ...
And ...
I'm an action hero.
Just like Ben and Lucy.

1 Look at the family tree and circle the words.

Jack is Nick's *grandfather*.
Julia is Nick's *grandmother*.
Claire and Ted are Nick's *parents*.
Oliver is Jack's *son*.
Claire is Julia's *daughter*.
Nick is Jack's *grandson*.
Penny is Julia's *granddaughter*.
Oliver is Nick's *uncle*.
Lisa is Nick's *aunt*.
Paula and Zoe are Nick's *cousins*.

1 Nick is Penny's *brother / father*.
2 Paula is Zoe's *cousin / sister*.
3 Ted is Penny's *uncle / father*.
4 Lisa is Paula's *mother / sister*.

2 Add the missing *'s* to each sentence. Say the sentences.

1 Tom is Simon father. ('s)
2 Simon is Tom son. ('s)

3 006 Watch, listen and say.

Language focus

This is Greg.
He's Gina**'s brother**.

And this is Gina.
She's Greg**'s sister**.

4 Draw and talk about your family.

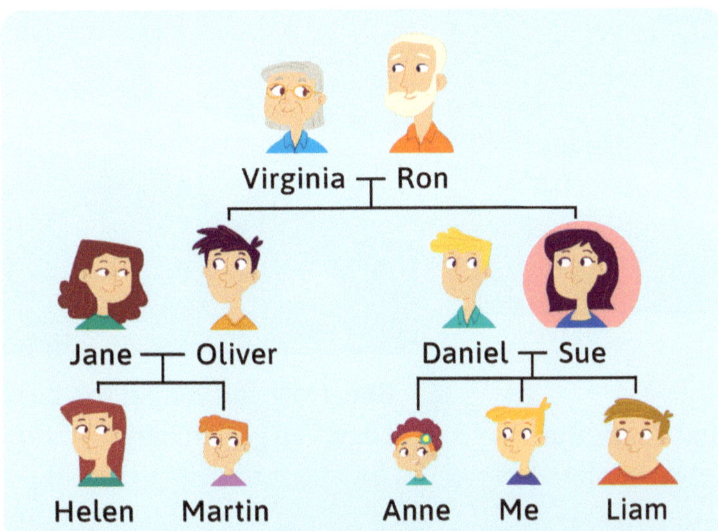

The old book

1 007 **Who's got the book in each picture?**

1

Lucy: What's that?
Ben: I think it's a door. A secret door.
Lucy: Let's open it. Buster, wait here!

2

Ben: Here's the book. It looks really old.
Zelda: They've got the book, Horax! Let's get them.
Horax: Wait a minute, Zelda!

3

Ben: I'm so happy we've got it!
Horax: Me too! You're good at finding things that I want!
Ben: Oh no! Who are they?

4

Horax: Give us the book! Tie Lucy up, Zelda.
Lucy: You can't keep the book. It's ours.
Horax: It's ours now! And all the treasure it brings.

5

Ben: Good dog, Buster!
Lucy: Hurry up, Buster, please.
Ben: Show us the way to Horax and Zelda, Buster.

6

Ben: How can we get the book back?
Lucy: I've got an idea!

Horax: Stop, you two!
Zelda: Go away, silly dog!
Lucy: Stop them, Buster!

Lucy: Run! We've got the book.
Ben: Well done, Buster!

2 **Write *t* (true) or *f* (false).**

1 Ben and Lucy go to the cellar. ☐
2 Buster finds the old book. ☐
3 Horax and Zelda are good people. ☐
4 Horax and Zelda want the book. ☐
5 Buster is a dog. ☐
6 Buster helps The Explorers to get the book back. ☐

Phonics

3 **Find who says …** Let's get them.

4 008 **Listen and say.**

Gus pats his pets a lot.

1 Our school

1 009 Listen and say the words. Then check with a friend.

1 English
2 Maths
3 Geography
4 Science
5 I.T.
6 Music
7 Art
8 P.E.
9 History

BIG QUESTION What kinds of puzzles are there?

2 010 Listen and correct the sentences.

1 Ben's favourite subject is History.
2 Lucy understands the puzzle.
3 Lucy wants to ask their Maths teacher.
4 Lucy doesn't like the librarian.

3 Ask and answer.

Do you like History?

Yes, I do. It's my favourite subject.

What subjects are you good at?

Music and Art. I'm very good at them.

1 011 Listen and write *Z* (Zoe) or *A* (Adam).

1 I love doing number puzzles. z

2 My sister likes number puzzles. ____

3 I like listening to stories. ____

4 My sister doesn't like writing stories. ____

5 I love singing. ____

6 I don't like listening to music. ____

2 Where do the words go? Say the sentences.

1 I love. (singing)

2 I don't like number puzzles. (doing)

3 She doesn't like stories. (writing)

4 She likes to music. (listening)

3 012 Watch, listen and say.

Language focus

I **like** listen**ing** to music.
I **like** climb**ing** trees.
I **love** sleep**ing** in the sun.
But I **don't like** hear**ing** bees.

He **likes** listen**ing** to music.
He **likes** climb**ing** trees.
He **loves** sleep**ing** in the sun.
But he **doesn't like** hear**ing** bees!

4 Play the *like / don't like* game.

doing number puzzles
listening to stories
singing
doing projects
learning about animals
listening to music
sleeping
writing stories

1 013 Listen and tick ☑ the subjects you hear. Then sing the song.

There are lots of puzzles
To find answers to.
They help us understand
What's false and what's true.

I love learning about the world
In Geography.
I love playing sports and games.
It's time to do P.E.

I love hearing about the past.
I love History.
Let's turn on our computers now.
It's time to do I.T.

I love doing lots of sums
And Maths is really cool.
Oh yeah! I love all the things
That we learn at school!

There are lots of puzzles …

2 Solve the puzzles and write the school subjects.

1 h l g E s n i

2 c c n e i S e

3 y t H r s i o

4 h o r p G e y g a

3 Create a puzzle for your friend.

1 Read and draw the missing picture.

Hi Julia

I know you are in my class this year. Here are some of the things we have to do: We have to wear a school uniform. We have to learn some new words every week. We have to arrive at school at nine o'clock. We have to put our homework book on the teacher's desk before the lesson. See you tomorrow!

John

2 Put the words in order. Say the sentences.

1 uniform. have to wear You a school

2 have to your homework put on the teacher's desk. You

3 Watch, listen and say.

015

Language focus

You **have to wear** a uniform. You **have to clean** your eyes like this.

You **have to climb** like me. You can't? I see. Hehe!

4 Read and play the rules game.

before you go to bed every day
before you go to school before you eat

wash your hands

brush your teeth

You have to brush your teeth before you go to bed.

have breakfast

get up

do your homework

1 016 Why can't Lucy and Ben read the book?

1

Lucy: Excuse me. Can you help us, please?
Mr Williams: Yes, of course. What's the problem?
Ben: We can't read this book. It's in code.

2

Mr Williams: Hmm. Let me think. It isn't easy. There are lots of clues in this book. But they're all in code. Very interesting! I like doing puzzles!

3

Mr Williams: This is difficult! Can I keep the book? I can tell you tomorrow.
Lucy: Keep the book?
Ben: No, sorry. We can't give it to you.

4

Mr Williams: OK then, sorry kids. I can't help you. I've got to go.
Lucy: OK, thanks anyway.

5

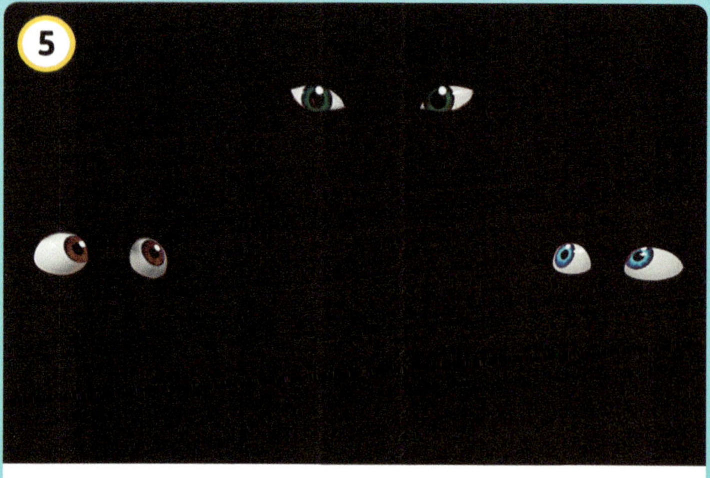

Ben: What's going on? It's dark!
Lucy: Come on, Ben. We have to get out of here.

6

Ben: Someone wants our book!
Lucy: It's probably Horax and Zelda.
Ben: What? Here in the school? No way!
Lucy: We have to find a way to read this code.

7

Lucy: Hey, look at this! What's this here?

Ben: Let me see. I think ... Yes, it's the secret to the code. Yes! Now we can read the clues.

8

Horax: The children have got the book.

Zelda: What about the code?

Horax: I don't understand the code, yet. We have to follow those kids.

2 Use the code to write the message from Lucy and Ben's book.

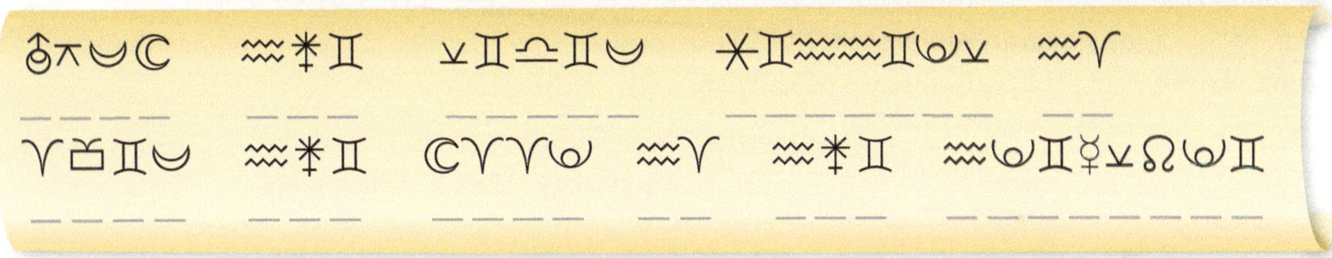

Phonics

3 Find who says ... OK, thanks anyway.

4 017 Listen and say.

DJ Cool K is on his way from the UK to the USA.

1 **Look at the pictures and the title. What do you think the story is about? Write three sentences.**

I think the story is about … There is / are …

2 **Read the story quickly. Try to find the answers.**

1 What is the teacher's name?
2 What doesn't Oliver like?
3 What do the children write down on the paper?

3 018 **Read and listen. Check your answers.**

Puzzles are great fun

All the girls and boys in Oliver's class like playing football but Oliver doesn't like football. Many of them love playing computer games but Oliver really doesn't like computer games. 'He's a bit silly!' a boy called Mike says.

At lunch Ms Sanders, their teacher, goes outside with her class. The children love that. Most of the children run around but Oliver prefers sitting under a tree. 'He likes thinking,' some children say. 'He's a bit silly!' Mike says.

One day, the children have a History lesson. Many of the children love History. They love listening to Ms Sanders' stories. Oliver finds listening to stories boring, he prefers numbers and dates.

Ms Sanders sees that Oliver is not listening and she stops her story. She goes to the board and writes a date on it: 10th August 1992.

'History is full of important dates.' Ms Sanders says. Oliver starts to listen. 'And dates are important in our lives too.' Ms Sanders says. 'Look at this date. It's very important to me but maybe it's not important to you. What do you think it is, Oliver?'

The children are all very quiet now. They are looking at Ms Sanders, and they are looking at Oliver. 'It's a Monday!' Oliver says.
'Ha ha!' laugh the children in the class.
Ms Sanders tells them to be quiet. 'You're right, Oliver! It is a Monday and it's my birthday. How do you know it's a Monday?'

'It's easy!' Oliver says. 'Write down a date. And I can tell you what day of the week it is!'
'That's not true!' Mike says. 'You can't know that! You're not a computer. Hahahaha!'

'Take out some paper,' Ms Sanders tells the class. 'Write down a day, a month and a year.'

The children put their papers in front of Oliver.
10th April 2016 – 'It's a Sunday!' Oliver says.
21st September 1999 – 'It's a Tuesday!' Oliver says.
1st January 2001 – 'It's a Monday!' Oliver says.
'Now let's look at the computer!' says Ms Sanders. 'Mike, come here!'
Mike sits down at the computer. He types the first date: 10th April 2016.
'It is a Sunday!' Mike says. He looks at the next date.
'It is a Tuesday!' Mike says. And when he looks at the next date he says, 'It is a Monday!'

'Wow!' the children say. 'You're a computer, Oliver!'
Oliver smiles. 'I'm not a computer!'
'Can you teach us how to do this?' Mike says.
'Mm. I've got an idea,' Oliver says. 'Let's start a puzzle club at our school. Puzzles are great fun!'
'Hooray!' the children shout.

4 Put the story in order.

- ☐ In a History lesson, Ms Sanders is telling a story.
- ☐ Oliver doesn't listen to the story.
- ☐ Oliver says the day of the week for each date.
- ☐ Oliver says what day of the week the date is.
- ☐ Ms Sanders writes a date on the board.
- ☐ The children start a puzzle club together.
- ☐ The children write down some dates on pieces of paper.

5 019 Listen to a summary of the story. Write the three differences.

In the summary we have …

1 Maths instead of History.
2 ______ instead of ______.
3 ______ instead of ______.

6 Talk together: What activities or subjects at school are fun for you?

I really like … *My favourite …* *I think it's fun to …*

GEOMETRICAL SHAPES

What shapes can we see in buildings?

Super fact!

Triangle shapes are often used in buildings because they are very strong.

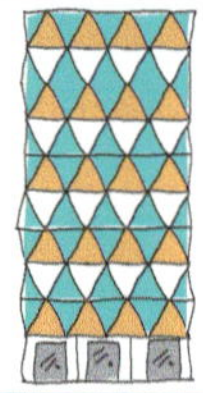

1 020 Listen and point.

pentagons

hexagons

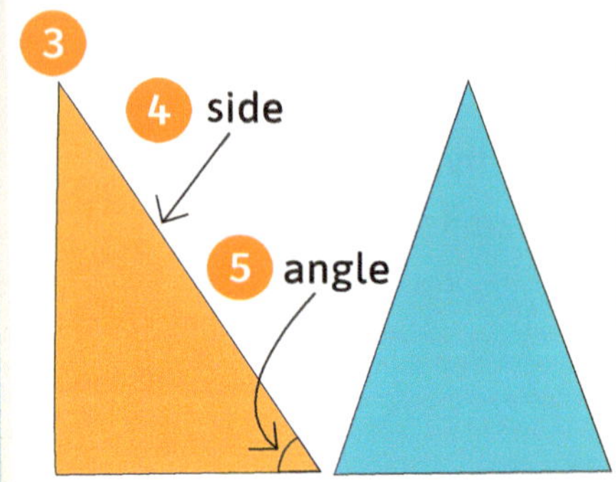

triangles

2 Look at these sequences. Draw the missing shapes.

1 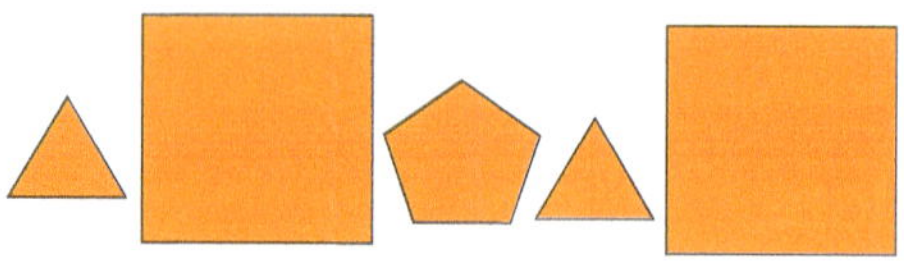 ____

2  ____

3 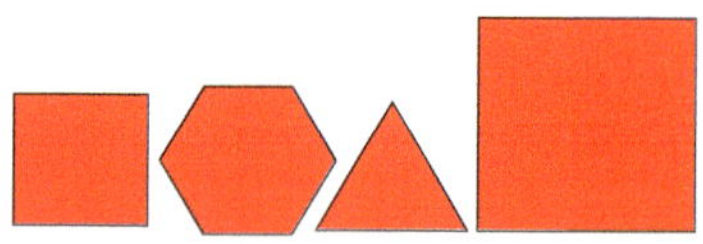 ____ 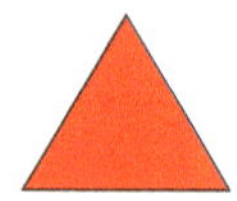

4  ____ 

3 What shape is it? Match the sentences with the shapes.

1 It's got five sides and five angles. ☐

2 It's got three sides and three angles. ☐

3 It's got six sides and six angles. ☐

4 It hasn't got any angles. ☐

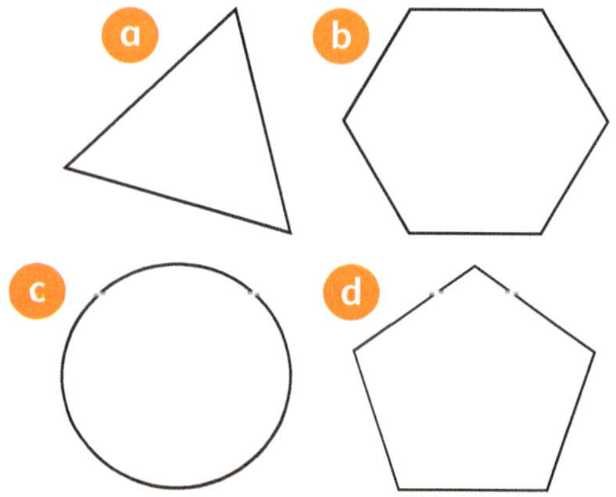

4 **Look at the butterfly puzzle and tell your partner how to colour the shapes.**

The kites are blue.

OK. And what colour are the small triangles?

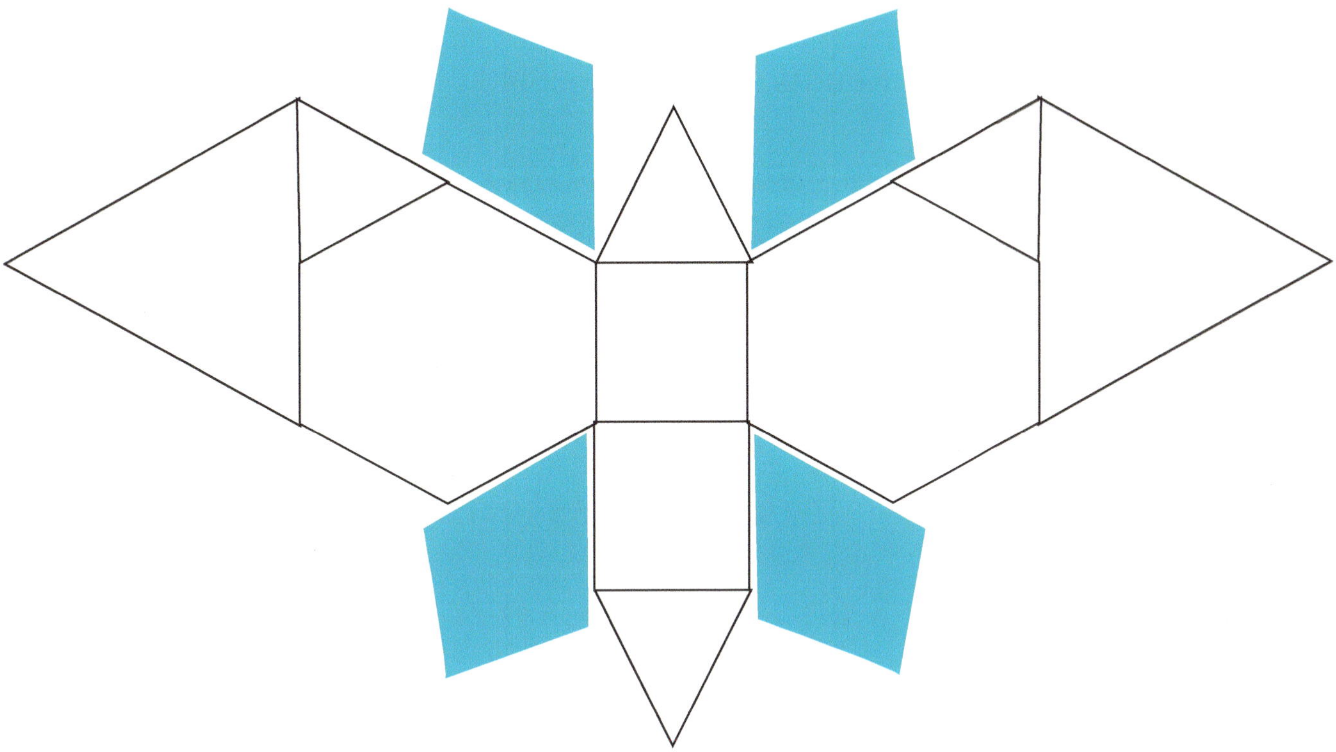

5 **Project** **Use shapes to draw an insect or a bird. Count the number of shapes, angles and sides. Tell your friends.**

This is my insect. It's a dragonfly. It's got six shapes: two hexagons, two squares, two pentagons, three triangles, three circles and four kites. There are … sides and … angles.

Talk and find out

Favourite subjects

1 **Make a prediction.**

I predict that my class's favourite school subject is ____________.

2 **Work in groups of four. Draw a table. Ask and write.**

Favourite subject	Names	
I.T.	Maria	1
English	Shelley, Joshua, Tom	3

3 **Add up all the answers from the groups on the board.**

Favourite subject	Groups	Total
I.T.	1 + 2	3
English	3 + 1	

4 **Make a bar chart and talk about the results.**

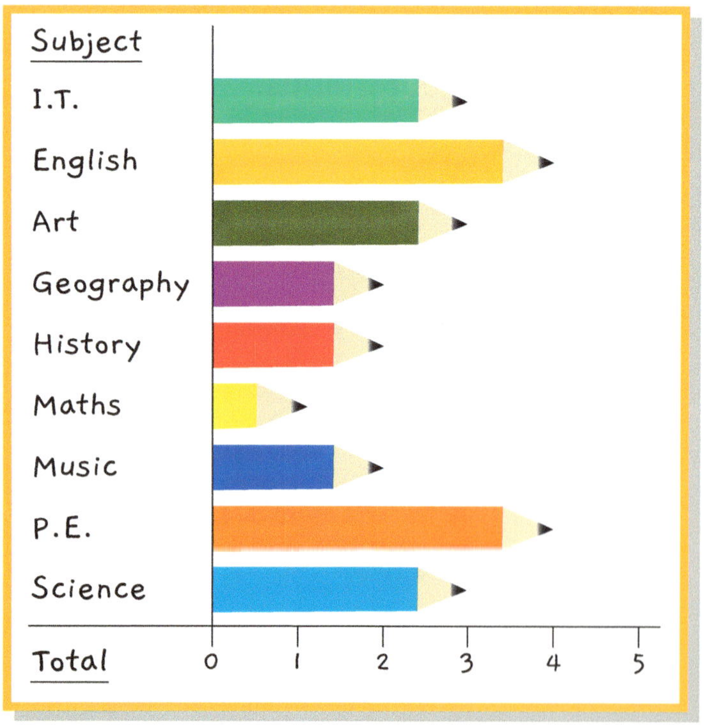

Was your prediction correct?

I predicted that my class's favourite school subject was …

Now I know that my class's favourite school subject is …

My portfolio

1 Read about the portfolio.

Did you know ... ?

Your portfolio helps you to show your learning progress. You can show:

- your stories and other things you write.
- project reports, bar charts, etc.

You can create a print portfolio or a digital portfolio.

In a print portfolio, you can take photos of your work and stick them to your portfolio.

In a digital portfolio, you can upload audio or video recordings of role-play activities and other conversations.

My portfolio

- My name: Noah
- My class: English
- My teacher's name: Peter
- My favourite colour: orange
- My favourite song: Mr Blue
- My favourite book: Super Minds
- I like eating: ice cream
- I like drinking: tea
- People in my family: my mother, my sister Jane, my dog Alf

MY PORTFOLIO

- **My name:** Noah
- **My class:** English
- **My teacher's name:** Peter
- **My favourite colour:** orange
- **My favourite song:** Mr Blue
- **My favourite book:** Super Minds
- I like eating: ice cream
- I like drinking: tea
- People in my family: my mother, my sister Jane, my dog Alf

2 Write a profile for your portfolio.

3 Write some rules for your English class.

Writing tip

Check your sentences for capital letters and full stops.

English class rules:

We have to speak English.
We have to do our homework.
We have to listen to ...
We have to read a book every ...

2 The picnic

1 Listen and say the words. Then check with a friend. (021)

1 apple juice
2 rolls
3 cheese
4 water
5 soup
6 vegetables
7 lemonade
8 salad

BIG QUESTION What's good to eat?

Near the village there's a pool. Look down deep where water's cool.

2 (022) **Listen and answer.**

1 What are Ben and Lucy looking for?
2 What does Lucy drink?
3 What does Ben eat?
4 Why is Buster barking?

3 **Ask and answer.**

I'm hungry / thirsty.

Would you like some ... ?

1 023 Listen and tick ✓ the roll.

2 Complete with *some* or *any*. Say the sentences.

1 Are there ________ tomatoes?

2 Yes, there are ________ tomatoes.

3 Is there ________ cheese?

4 No, there isn't ________ cheese.

3 024 Watch, listen and say.

Language focus

Is there **any** food in your bag?
Yes, there is **some** food.
Is there **any** cheese in your bag?
No, there isn't **any** cheese.

Are there **any** rolls in your bag?
No, there aren't **any** rolls.
Are there **any** apples in your bag?
Yes, there are **some** apples.

4 Play the imaginary sandwich game.

1 025 **Listen and match the food. Then sing the song.**

1

2

3

a
 ☐
b
 ☐
c
 ☐

Is there any lemonade?
In your soup today?
Mix it in, eat it all,
Then go out and play.

Good idea, good idea!
That sounds good to me!
Good idea, good idea!
I'm so hungry!

Is there any apple juice
In your salad too?
Mix it in, eat it all
That's my lunch for you.

Good idea, good idea! ...

Are there any vegetables
In your jam roll, please?
Mix them in, eat them all
With a piece of cheese.

Good idea, good idea! ...

2 **What do you think is good? Complete the table.**

	Good	Bad
In a roll	chicken	water
In a salad		
In soup		

3 **Compare with a partner.**

Chicken is good in a roll.

Water is bad in a roll.

1 027 Listen and tick ✓ the food in the soup.

2 Put the words in order. Say the sentences.

1 we | Shall | in the soup? | some carrots | put

2 And | how | onions? | some | about

3 028 Watch, listen and say.

Language focus

It's six o'clock and time to eat!
How about some peas?
Or **shall we have** some bread with cheese?
I'd like some flies, and that's all, please.

4 Make a bowl of soup or a salad with a friend.

The golden apple

1 029 Why is Buster ill?

1

Lucy: Buster. Buster, what's the matter?

Ben: Lucy, look, a snake. It bit Buster. Let's take him to the village. It's not far.

Lucy: Let's go now. Come on.

2

Lucy: Can you help us? A snake bit our dog.

Ben: He's very ill. Have you got any medicine?

Woman: No, but go to the old man in the hut next to the big tree. He can help you.

3

Man: Take your dog to the top of the mountain. There's a waterfall there. Above it, there's a tree with a golden apple. Your dog has to eat that apple.

4

Horax: Quick. I want to get to that apple first. We don't want Buster to get better!

Lucy: Look, Ben, there are Horax and Zelda.

5

Lucy: Look at the tree. It's Horax and Zelda.

Ben: Hey, Horax. Stop!

Zelda: Do you want any help, Horax?

Horax: No. I think I've got it.

6

Zelda: Horax, you fool!

Ben: Thanks for the apple, Horax!

7

Ben: Lucy, look. There's a letter.
Lucy: It's an *I*, Ben. It's our first letter.
Ben: Shall we write it in the book?
Lucy: Good idea.

8

Lucy: Bye, Horax. Bye, Zelda.
Ben: And thanks again for the apple.
Zelda: You kids. Just you wait!

2 **Write *t* (true) or *f* (false).**

1 Lucy and Ben take Buster to a village. ☐
2 A woman tells Ben and Lucy about the waterfall. ☐
3 The apple tree is under a waterfall. ☐
4 The kids have to find a silver apple. ☐
5 Horax gets to the tree first. ☐
6 Lucy finds the letter in a pool near the waterfall. ☐

Phonics

3 **Find who says …** Shall we write it in the book?

4 030 **Listen and say.**

I like my little fish and ice cream pie!

Skills

1 031 **Listen and answer the questions.**

1 What time does lunch start?
At __________ o'clock

2 Where do the children eat?
In the __________ hall

3 Which children eat first?
Children with __________

4 What is Lisa's favourite school lunch?
__________, peas and chips

5 When does Lisa have sandwiches?
On __________

6 What time does lunch finish?
At __________ o'clock

2 **Read and match. There is one extra plate of food.**

Connor ☐
My favourite meal is chicken with rice and salad.

☐ Holly
My favourite meal is a cheese sandwich with tomato and egg.

Thomas ☐
My favourite meal is sausages and green beans.

☐ Grace
My favourite meal is fish with potatoes and carrots.

1

2

3

4

5

3 **Tell your friend about meals at your school.**

Lunch starts at …

My favourite meal is …

1 Read the poem and tick ✓ the food the girl eats for each meal.

Breakfast is the meal
At the start of the day.
Sausage, toast and egg
Then I'm on my way.

Lunch is the meal
In the middle of the day.
A sandwich and some milk
On my school lunch tray.

Dinner is the meal
Near the end of the day.
Chicken, rice and beans
Then I'm off to play.

breakfast	✓							
lunch								
dinner								

2 Complete the poem about you.

Breakfast is the meal
At the start of the day.
____
Then I'm on my way.

Lunch is the meal
In the middle of the day.
____
On my school lunch tray.

Dinner is the meal
Near the end of the day.
____
Then I'm off to play.

Edible plants

What plant parts are good to eat?

Super fact!
A tomato is not a vegetable – it's a fruit!

1 032 Listen and point.

2 Read and put ticks ✓ in the table.

We make juice from fruit. We can also make delicious fruit puddings.

Asparagus is a stem. It tastes good in a soup.

Carrots are roots. They taste good in soups and salads.

Do you like eating leaves? We often eat lettuce leaves in salads.

Sometimes we eat the seeds of plants, like peas. We can eat them with meat or fish.

	roots	stems	leaves	seeds	fruit
asparagus		✓			
carrot					
lettuce					
orange					
pea					

3 Which food and drink isn't from a plant part?

1	potato	onion	cheese	banana
2	tomato juice	water	lemonade	watermelon
3	carrot salad	asparagus soup	lettuce	chicken

4 033 Listen. Match the animals with their food.

5 Project Draw a picnic with food and drink from plant parts. Write sentences about the picnic food.

We make the orange juice from fruit.

We make the salad from leaves and roots.

Talk and find out

At the sandwich shop

1 Choose a role card. Read and plan.

The SANDWICH SHOP

The BEST sandwiches in town

Choose any fillings:

Student A

- You are at a sandwich shop.
- Choose three fillings for your sandwich.
- Order a sandwich and a drink.

Student B

- You make sandwiches at a sandwich shop.
- Ask the teacher which fillings you have and circle them.
- Find out what your customer wants to eat.

2 Act out your play.

Useful language

Sandwich maker	Customer
Can I help you?	I'd like a … , please.
Sorry, we haven't got any …	Have you got any … ?
How about … ?	I like … a lot.
Here you are.	Can I have … ?

My favourite foods

1 Think of all the words you know for food and drink. Write them on bits of paper.

pineapple · cherries · chicken · orange juice · pizza · coffee · sausages · sandwich

2 How many groups can you put your words in? Colour each group.

orange juice · coffee

cherries · pineapple

chicken · sausages

pizza · sandwich

3 Write your words in lists.

My favourites	I like	I don't like	I really don't like
sausages orange juice chicken	cherries	pizza sandwiches	coffee pineapple

Writing tip

Remember to use apostrophes for contractions.

do + not = don't

I + have = I've

4 Write about a meal you would like and a meal you would not like. Add photos or drawings.

My favourite meal is sausages with chips and peas, apple juice to drink and cherries.

I don't like fish with onions and tomatoes. I don't like pineapple and I don't like coffee. Ugh!

3 Daily tasks

1 Listen and say the words. Then check with a friend.

1 sweep
2 wash up
3 do the shopping
4 tidy up
5 cook
6 dry the dishes
7 take the dog for a walk
8 feed the dog

BIG QUESTION What's it like to work at night?

Helping hands,
there's work to do.
A letter's here.
It waits for you.

2 Listen and correct the sentences.

1 The boy calls the dog 'Buster'.
2 Buster is still feeling ill.
3 Lucy doesn't like cooking.
4 Ben likes washing up.

3 Play the mime game.

Are you drying the dishes?

Yes, I am.

1 036 Listen and number.

a 

b 

c 

d 

e 

f 

2 Look at Activity 1 again and write *quarter* or *half*. Say the sentences.

1  I do my homework at ________ past five.

2  I wash up at ________ past six.

3  I take the dog for a walk at ________ to seven.

4  I go to bed at ________ past eight.

3 037 Watch, listen and say.

Language focus

 I get out of bed at **half past** seven.

 I get dressed at eight **o'clock**.

 I have my breakfast at **quarter past** eight.

 I get my bag at **quarter to** nine.

4 Play the time game.

1 038 Listen and draw the times on the clocks. Then sing the song.

I get up. It's quarter to three.
I get dressed and have some tea.
I feed my dog. I sweep the floor.
It's nine o'clock, I'm at my door.

You can only get to the moon at night
And I'm the pilot of the night time flight.
Let's go to the moon!

I'm in my spaceship. It's half past nine.
I'm the pilot and I feel fine.
It's half past ten, we're on the moon.
Take some photos. It's time to leave soon.

You can only get to the moon at night ...

I'm now back home. It's half past three.
I walk the dog then I have my tea.
Wash up the dishes – in bed very soon.
Time to sleep and then back to the moon.

You can only get to the moon at night ...

10, 9, 8, 7, 6, 5, 4, 3, 2, 1 ... BLAST OFF!

2 Read and correct the sentences.

1 The pilot gets up after three o'clock.
2 At quarter past nine the pilot is in her spaceship.
3 The pilot gets to the moon after eleven o'clock.
4 The pilot never flies at night.

3 Compare with a partner.

get up | leave the house | get home | go to bed

I get up at half past seven.

I don't. I get up at quarter to eight.

1 Read. Put ticks ☑ or crosses ☒ in the table.

How I help my mum and dad

by Nick, aged 9

- I always take the dog for a walk. I do that on Mondays, Tuesdays, Wednesdays, Thursdays and Fridays after school. I love my dog!
- I usually dry the dishes. I do that on Mondays, Tuesdays, Thursdays and Fridays.
- I sometimes do the washing up. I do the washing up on Tuesdays and Thursdays. I don't really like washing up!
- I never cook. Never! I want to cook but Mum says I can't.

	Monday	Tuesday	Wednesday	Thursday	Friday
walk the dog					
dry the dishes					
wash up					
cook					

2 Where do the words go? Say the sentences.

1 I tidy up on Saturdays. (always)
2 I help Mum to do the shopping. (usually)
3 I take the dog for a walk at 6 o'clock. (sometimes)
4 I go to bed before 8 o'clock. (never)

3 Watch, listen and say. 040

Language focus

Gina **always** climbs this beautiful tree.
Greg **usually** climbs the tree with me.
Gina **sometimes** sleeps on top of the tree.
But Greg **never** sleeps there next to me.

4 Play the true or false game.

Nick sometimes walks his dog after school. True or false?

False. He always walks his dog after school.

Tidying up

1 041 What does Zelda think of the village?

1

Ben: So what does the next clue mean?
Lucy: Well, the letter's in this village. But where?
Ben: Let's look for it tomorrow morning. It's quarter past nine and I'm tired.

2

Horax: It's here. The next letter is in this village.
Zelda: Let's wait for dark.
Horax: Good idea. We can look for it after dark.

3

Horax: It isn't here.
Zelda: I'm tired and I don't like this village. It's half past ten. Let's go soon.

4

Ben: Oh no! What a mess!
Lucy: 'Helping hands', remember the clue.
Ben: Yes, maybe this is what we have to do before we find the next letter.

5

Ben: This table is heavy! There's no letter here.

6

Lucy: Why do I always get the horrible jobs? Where is that letter? We have to find it soon!

Lucy: What's that? Yes! Ben, come here!
Ben: What is it?
Lucy: I've got something to show you.

Ben: Wow! It's the next letter.
Lucy: The letter *F*. Now we've got our second letter!

2 Answer the questions.

Who …

1 wants to look for the clue in the morning? __________

2 listens to the kids talk about the clue? __________

3 doesn't like the village? __________

4 lifts the table up? __________

5 tidies up the rubbish? __________

6 finds the next letter? __________

Phonics

3 Find who says …

The letter *F*. Now we've got our second letter!

4 042 Listen and say.

Vic sells fabulous fans from the back of his van.

1 **Look at the pictures and write *t* (true) or *f* (false).**

1 The shoemaker's job is difficult. ______
2 The elves cut leather for the shoes. ______
3 One night, the shoemaker sees six elves. ______
4 The elves make the small trousers and shirts. ______

2 043 **Read and listen. Check your answers.**

The Shoemaker and the elves

In a country far away there is a shoemaker. His job is not easy. He always gets up at 6 o'clock and he never goes to bed before 11 o'clock. The shoemaker always cuts the leather and then he makes the shoes. He works a lot, but he hasn't got a lot of money. One day he cuts the leather for ten pairs of shoes. But he is very tired, so he leaves the leather on the kitchen table and goes to bed.

The next morning, the shoemaker gets up and sees ten pairs of beautiful shoes on the kitchen table. He is very happy. That night, before he goes to bed, the shoemaker cuts the leather for twenty pairs of shoes and leaves it on the kitchen table. The next morning there are twenty pairs of beautiful shoes on the table. Every night, he leaves the leather for more pairs of shoes, and every morning there are beautiful shoes on the table!

Many people in the town want a pair of the shoes and soon the shoemaker has got a lot of money. But who is making the shoes? The shoemaker wants to know. One night he hides under a table and waits. At 12 o'clock the shoemaker sees five elves. They jump onto the table and start making the shoes. The shoemaker sees their clothes too. They are very old and not very nice. At 5 o'clock in the morning the elves stop and leave the house.

The shoemaker wants to say 'thank you' to the elves, so he makes five beautiful small pairs of trousers and shirts. That night, he leaves the clothes on the table with the leather. In the morning the clothes are gone, but the leather is still there.
First, the shoemaker is sad. 'The elves are not making shoes for me anymore!' he thinks. But then he thinks, 'It's great. The elves have beautiful, new clothes and I have a good life now.'

3 **Complete the sentences with words from the story.**

1 The shoemaker gets up …
2 When the shoemaker goes to bed, he is …
3 In the morning he finds …
4 The next night he leaves leather …
5 Everyone in town wants …
6 The elves start work at …
7 The shoemaker makes clothes to say …
8 The shoemaker is happy because …

4 044 **Listen to a summary of the story. Write the three differences.**

In the summary we have …

1 five instead of ten pairs of shoes.
2 ________ instead of ____________________.
3 ________ instead of ____________________.

5 **Ask the elves to help you.**

Elves, please do my homework tonight.

Elves, please tidy my room tonight.

JOBS AT *night*

What jobs can people do at night?

Super fact!

People feel very tired at 2 o'clock in the morning and 2 o'clock in the afternoon.

1 045 Listen and point.

1 fire fighter

2 police officer

3 ambulance driver

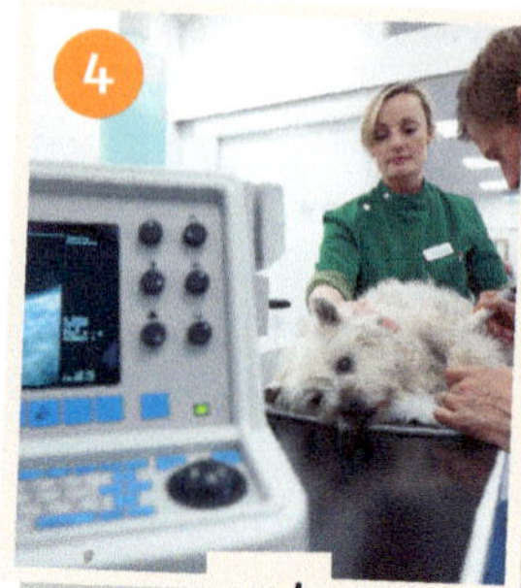
4 vet

5 cleaner

2 Read and write the jobs in the table.

Job	What they do at night
1 ____________________	This person cleans the town.
2 ____________________	This person takes ill people to hospital.
3 ____________________	This person stops fires.
4 ____________________	This person looks after animals.
5 ____________________	This person helps people.

3 046 Listen and check your answers.

4 What's it like to work at night? Circle your answers. Write one more sentence about working at night.

1 Working at night is fun / difficult.

2 It's easy / not easy to sleep in the day.

3 You see / don't see your family every day.

4 You can do more things / need to sleep in the day.

5 ____

5 **Read Anna's work diary and write times under the pictures.**

1 ______ 2 ______ 3 ______ 4 ______

An Ambulance Driver's Diary

NIGHT

7 o'clock – I eat lunch – My family are finishing dinner. It's dark outside.

10 o'clock – My family are asleep – I start work. Work is always very busy.

3 o'clock – I have dinner in the hospital.

DAY

6 o'clock – The sun is coming up. I finish work and go home.

8 o'clock – My family have breakfast. I'm usually very tired and I go to sleep.

4 o'clock – My children come home from school. I get up and have breakfast. Sometimes I tidy up the house.

5 o'clock – I usually help my children with their homework then I go for a walk.

6 **Make sentences about Anna's routine. Use *always*, *sometimes* or *never*.**

She always goes home at six o'clock.

She never has breakfast at seven o'clock.

7 **Project** **Choose a job that people do at night. Write a diary for their day or night.**

A Police Officer's Diary

Night

6 o'clock – I wake up and have breakfast.

7 o'clock – I feed the dog and then I cycle to work.

9 o'clock – I usually have a break and drink some tea.

12 o'clock – I have a sandwich for lunch.

5 o'clock – I finish work and I sometimes have dinner with the other police officers.

Talk and find out

Helping at home

1 **Make a prediction.**

I predict that there are ________ children in my class who sometimes __________.

2 **Read and tick ☑ *Yes* or *No*.**

	Yes / No
1 Do you sometimes cook?	☐ / ☐
2 Do you sometimes wash up?	☐ / ☐
3 Do you sometimes tidy your room?	☐ / ☐
4 Do you sometimes dry the dishes?	☐ / ☐
5 Do you sometimes help with the shopping?	☐ / ☐
6 Do you sometimes wash your clothes?	☐ / ☐

3 **Ask and answer.**

Who sometimes cooks?

4 **Make a table and write a report.**

	Yes	No		Yes	No
	12	9		17	4
	15	6		14	7
	18	3		7	14

I predicted that there are 10 children who sometimes cook at home. Now I know that there are 12 children who sometimes cook at home and there are 9 children who never cook at home.

My family

1 Write a list of things people in your family do.

my mum	my sister	I
works on the computer	goes to school	go to ...

2 Underline each word in your list in a colour to show how often people do it.

always usually sometimes

3 What do the people in your family do at the weekend?

My mum always works on the computer.
My sister never makes breakfast ...
I sometimes go to ...

4 Write a poem and add photos or drawings. Use the text to help you.

I always go to school on Mondays,
I usually ... on Tuesdays,
I sometimes ... on Wednesdays,
I like doing things that way.
I always ... on Thursdays,
I usually ... on Fridays,
But I never ... at the weekend,
Because that's the time to play.

Writing tip

Poems are nice if they rhyme.

4 Around town

1 047 Listen and say the words. Then check with a friend.

1 bank
2 tower
3 funfair
4 library
5 market square
6 supermarket
7 bus station
8 car park
9 sports centre
10 map

BIG QUESTION What do we find in towns?

Go up high in the town. See the letter when you look down.

2 048 Listen and answer.

1 Where do Ben and Lucy want to go?
2 Who do they ask?
3 Where is the tower?
4 What does the woman tell them to look at?

3 Look at the map. Ask and answer.

Where is the shoe shop?

It's next to the car park, between the bus station and the sports centre.

1 Look, read and draw lines.

a 

c 

1 The school is opposite the park.
2 The clock is above the window.
3 The map is near the library.
4 The clock is below the window.

b 

d 

2 Where do the words go? Say the sentences.

1 The bus stop is the supermarket. (near)
2 The car park is the library. (opposite)
3 The clock is the map. (above)
4 The bus station is the tower. (below)

3 Watch, listen and say.

049

Language focus

The library is over there.
It's **opposite** the park, **near** the bank.
Below the sports centre there's a door.
The library's **above** it, on the second floor.

4 Play the guessing game.

I'm thinking of a place. It's opposite the bank. What is it?

I think it's the funfair.

That's right!

1 050 **Listen and write the two places the singer cannot find. Then sing the song.**

1 ______________ 2 ______________

Opposite the library,
In the square,
I'm looking for the bank
But it's not there.

Just below the tower,
Near the shop,
My map says there's a café
But there is not.

In front of the station,
In the street,
There's a place
Where people always meet.

I'm waiting here,
For Jennifer and Kate,
But they're already
Three hours late.

Excuse me, can you help me find my way?
I'm getting lost everywhere I go today.
I don't really understand this town.
Of course you don't,
Your map is upside down!

2 **Play the town game.**

Close your eyes. Imagine you can see a town. There's a big library. What's near it?

Near the library there's an old school. You close your eyes. Imagine the old school. What's opposite it?

3 **Draw and write about your imaginary town.**

1 052 Listen and number.

a

b

c

d

2 Put the words in order. Say the sentences.

1 buy the shop I'm going to to some bread.
2 I'm to basketball. the sports centre play going to

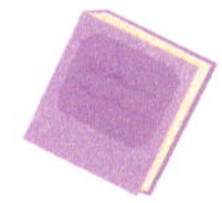

3 Watch, listen and say. 053

Language focus

I'm **going to** the library **to get** a book.
I'm **going to** the market **to get** some food.
I'm **going to** the station **to go** away
On a holiday, a super holiday!

4 Where are you going? Complete the sentences. Then act out.

1 I'm going to the market ___to buy___ some apples.
2 I'm going to the sports centre __________ swimming.
3 I'm going to my friend's house __________ a DVD.
4 I'm going to the library __________ a book.
5 I'm going to the supermarket __________ a T-shirt.
6 I'm going to my grandma's __________ in the kitchen.

to read	~~to buy~~
to go	to buy
to watch	to help

1 054 What is higher than the tower?

1

Zelda: They're going to the tower.
Lucy: Let's hurry, Ben. The tower's near the market square.
Ben: OK. Come on, Buster.

2

Lucy: Look, the tower's over there, near the school. The next letter's waiting for us!
Ben: Wow! There's a funfair!

3

Ben: Let's go to the funfair.
Lucy: Sorry, Ben. We're going to the tower to get the next letter. No time to play!

4

Ben: Come on, Lucy!
Lucy: Mmm. The tower is high ... but the Pirate Ship is higher.

5

Ben: Lucy! Where are you going?
Lucy: I'm going to the funfair to get the next letter!
Ben: What?

6

Lucy: Let's go on the Pirate Ship. Quick!
Ben: The Pirate Ship?

Ben: We're above the tower!
Lucy: Yes, we're really high now. It's scary!
Ben: There's the letter. Look!
Lucy: It's an *R*. Great!

Horax: Oh no!
Zelda: We're in the wrong place!

2 **Read and find the pictures in the story. Then answer.**

1 Find a picture where someone is excited. What makes them excited? ______
2 Find a picture where someone is scared. What are they scared of? ______
3 Find a picture where someone is angry. What makes them angry? ______
4 Find a picture where someone is happy. What makes them happy? ______

Phonics

3 **Find who says …** It's an *R*. Great!

4 055 **Listen and say.**

Rory, Reery and Rury – robots in a far away supermarket.

1 Look and read the sentences. Write words.

market

map

bus stop

castle

bank

sports centre

library

car park

1 People go there to get money. __________
2 It's old, and often next to a town. __________
3 This is a place where you go to find interesting books. __________
4 It's a good place to buy fruit and vegetables. __________
5 You go there to play football and basketball, and go swimming. __________
6 You need it in a town when you are new. It helps you to find places. __________

1 056 **Listen and find out where the robots are going. Write *C* (Caroline), *M* (Mark), *E* (Elly) and *R* (Robert).**

2 **Ask and answer.**

Where's Caroline going?

She's going to the café.

Why?

To get a salad.

3 **Imagine a robot. Write where he/she is going and why.**

This is Roro. He is going to the car park to get his super sports car.

TALL BUILDINGS

Why are some buildings tall?

Super fact!

The world's first skyscraper is in Chicago, USA. They finished building it in 1885.

1 057 Listen and point.

lighthouse

skyscraper

airport tower

clock tower

2 **Read and write the names of the buildings.**

1 The people in this building can see planes flying, landing and moving around the airport. They talk to the pilots and tell them when they can land their planes. __________

2 This building is by the sea. At night, ships can't see the land, but they can see the light at the top of this building. The light shows the ships where to go. __________

3 This big building is usually in a city. There can be flats, banks and shops in this building. __________

4 This building can be in a city or a town. The building tells people what time it is. __________

3 **Look at the buildings in Activity 1 again. Why do you think they're tall? Choose a, b, or c.**

It's tall …

a so that people can see the building from far away.

b so that people can see lots of things outside the building.

c so that there can be lots of things inside the building.

The lighthouse is tall so that …

4 **Why do you think these buildings are tall?**

I think building 1 is tall so that …

1

2

3

5 **What tall buildings are in your town? Why do you think they are tall?**

There's a … in my town. It's tall so that …

6 **Project** **Design a tall building. Describe it and say why it's tall. Tell your friends.**

This is a skyscraper. It's very tall so that there can be lots of things inside it. There are flats and shops. There's a swimming pool, too!

Talk and find out

Help a visitor in your town

1 Choose a role card. Read and plan.

Student A

You are visiting a town.
Ask the way to one of these places:

- the bank
- the sports centre
- the castle
- the library
- the train station

Ask a boy/girl from the town.

Student B

You live in the town.
Think about where these places are:

- the bank
- the sports centre
- the castle
- the library
- the train station

Tell the visitor where the place is.

Useful language

Visitor

Excuse me. Can you help me, please?
Where's the … ?
Thank you. That's very kind.

Boy/Girl

Yes, of course.
I'm sorry. I don't know.
No problem! The … is opposite / next to / below / between the …
You're welcome!

2 Act out your play.

Where's the … ?

It's …

Messages

1 Use the code to find out what the messages mean.

2 Imagine you are in a town. Write where you are at the different times.

9 o'clock: I'm in the library.
10 o'clock: I'm in the café.
11 o'clock: I'm in the shoe shop.
12 o'clock: I'm in the bank.
2 o'clock: I'm going home.

3 People are writing you text messages. Write their messages and your answers.

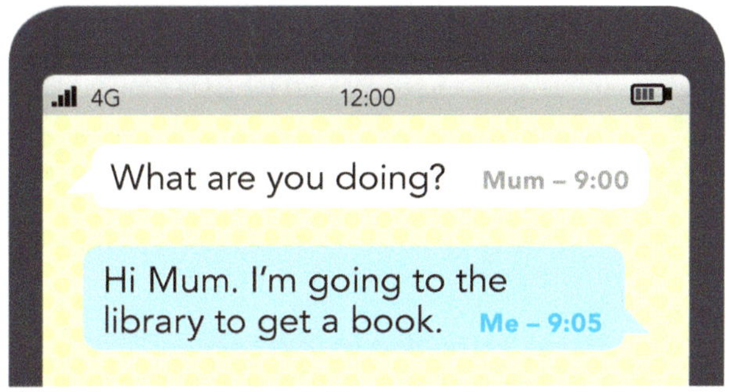

Writing tip

Remember that text messages can be very short!

5 Under the sea

1 058 Listen and say the words. Then check with a friend.

1 dolphin
2 seal
3 turtle
4 octopus
5 anchor
6 starfish
7 shell
8 seahorse

BIG QUESTION What's in the sea?

By diving down and getting wet, another letter you will get.

2 059 Listen and correct the sentences.

1 Ben doesn't like the sea.
2 Lucy thinks the letter is under the sea.
3 The children think the octopus is ugly.
4 Lucy is worried about Horax and Zelda.

3 Play the chain game.

There's a shark in the swimming pool.

There's a shark and a seahorse in the swimming pool.

1 060 Listen, read and write the missing words.

The golden toad

Many years ago in the forests of Costa Rica there were many golden toads. There were beautiful pools in the forest. These pools were the (1) __________ for the babies of the golden toads. 1987 was very hot. Soon, there was no (2) __________ in the pools. Now there are no more golden toads.

The megalodon

Megalodons were sharks. They were very, very (3) __________. They weren't very fast. Three million years ago the seas got colder. There wasn't any (4) __________ for the megalodons. Two million years ago there were no more megalodons.

2 Where do the words go? Say the sentences.

1 The golden toad from Costa Rica. (was)
2 Before 1987, it so hot. (wasn't)
3 Megalodons very fast swimmers. (weren't)
4 They very big and very heavy. (were)

3 061 Watch, listen and say.

Language focus

Greg **was** on a beach.
There **weren't** any people.
But then there **were** bees.
Then he **wasn't** happy.

4 Talk about the dinosaurs.

grey big brown blue small orange

It was small …

1 062 **Listen and tick ☑ the sea creatures that are in the song. Then sing the song.**

Deep under the dark, blue sea,
In between the rocks,
There was an awful animal,
Its name was Crocorox.

Swim, swim, swim, swim, swim away.
Swim away from here!
The Crocorox is dangerous.
The Crocorox is near!
Bad old Crocorox.

Its face was square and ugly,
Its eyes were small and red.
Its teeth were long and horrible,
There were scales on its head.

Swim, swim, swim ...

The starfish were all very scared,
The octopus was sad.
The turtle hid inside its shell,
That Crocorox was bad.

Help!
Swim, swim, swim, swim, swim away.
Swim away right now!
The Crocorox is hungry,
The Crocorox is ... Ow!

2 **Play the memory game.**

Its eyes were blue.

No, they weren't. They were red.

1 064 Look, listen and draw lines. Who ate the cake?

Sally
Bob
Spike
Alice
Sue
Judy
Tim

____

2 Match the questions and answers.

1 Were you in the sea, Julia?
2 Was Paul on the beach?
3 Where were you, Fred?
4 Were there shells on the beach?
5 Was there a shark in the sea?

a I was in the sea.
b No, there wasn't.
c Yes, there were.
d No, I wasn't.
e Yes, he was.

3 065 Watch, listen and say.

Language focus

Were you on the beach, Greg?
Yes, I **was**.
Were you in the sea, Greg?
No, I **wasn't**.

Were there turtles?
No, there **weren't**.
Was there a shark?
No, there **wasn't**.

4 Play the guessing game.

Guess where I was yesterday at five?

Were you in the park?

The trap

1 066 Which animal chases Horax?

1

Lucy: I can't see a letter.
Ben: What about that giant shell over there?
Lucy: Good idea. Maybe the letter's in there.
Ben: Let's have a look.

2

Lucy: Hurry up, Ben. Is there a letter there?
Ben: No, I don't think so.
Lucy: Let's look in a different place.

3

Ben: Help, Lucy! I can't get my arm out. I'm stuck.
Lucy: I'm sorry, Ben. I can't open the shell.

4

Ben: Oh no! It's Horax and Zelda.
Lucy: And a shark! I'm scared.
Horax: Come out, my beauty.

5

Zelda: I don't think the shark is very happy with us, Horax.
Horax: What! Not me, you stupid shark. The children. Get the children!

6

Horax: Help! Help!
Ben: That shark doesn't like Horax.
Lucy: No. I don't think he was happy in Horax's cage.

7

Ben: Thank you, octopus. You're very helpful.
Lucy: Finally. Now we can go and find that letter.

8

Lucy: Look! Look at the fish.
Ben: It's the letter *S*!
Lucy: Now we've got our fourth letter.

2 **Read and draw lines to make sentences.**

1 Lucy and Ben
2 Ben
3 Horax
4 The shark
5 The octopus
6 The fish

a has got a shark in a cage.
b helps Ben escape.
c gets stuck in a big shell.
d make the letter S.
e are looking for the letter.
f doesn't like Horax and Zelda.

Phonics

3 **Find who says ...**

I'm sorry, Ben. I can't open the shell.

4 067 **Listen and say.**

Shane is super scared. There's a shark in the swimming pool.

1 **Look at the pictures and the title. What do you think the story is about? Write three sentences. Share them with the class.**

I think the story is about … There is / are …

2 068 **Read and listen. Check your answers.**

Saved by dolphins

Kylie Morgan is on holiday with her mum and dad on the North Island of New Zealand.

One morning, her dad asks, 'Who wants to go for a swim in the sea?'

'I do!' says Kylie.

'I want to sit on the beach and read my book,' says her mum.

Kylie and her dad are swimming in the sea.

'Look!' shouts Kylie. 'There's a dolphin.'

Soon, there are four big dolphins in the water next to them. They are swimming in circles around Kylie and her dad.

'I think they want to play with us,' says Kylie.

The circle of dolphins gets smaller and smaller. They are now very close to Kylie and her dad. Then, the dolphins start to hit their tails on the top of the water. Up and down, up and down.

'This is fun,' laughs Kylie. But her dad is worried. 'Why are the dolphins doing this?' he thinks. But he doesn't say anything to Kylie.

Then he sees something. Behind the dolphins, there is a big, grey fin swimming through the water. Kylie's dad knows what it is. It's the fin of a great white shark.

Great white sharks can be very big and they have hundreds of teeth in their huge mouths. They can swim very fast, and they eat other sea animals like fish, seals, turtles and birds.

Kylie's dad knows all this. That is why he is scared. He pulls Kylie close to him but he still doesn't say anything.

For ten minutes, Kylie's dad watches the fin swimming around them. Then it swims away. The dolphins stop swimming in circles and Kylie and her dad can swim back to the beach.

On the beach, Kylie's dad tells Kylie and her mum about the shark.

'Those dolphins really helped us!' he says.

FACT FILE:
Great white shark

- They can grow ________.
- They have ________.
- They can swim ________.
- They eat ________.

3 **Complete the sentences.**

1 Kylie __Morgan__ is with her parents on holiday.
2 Kylie's mum doesn't want to go for a ________.
3 Kylie sees some ________ in the sea.
4 Kylie's dad doesn't tell her about the ________.
5 The shark stays near them for ________.
6 Kylie's dad thinks the dolphins ________ them.

4 069 **Listen to a summary of the story. Write the four differences.**

In the summary we have …

1 __sleeps__ instead of __reads her book__.
2 ________ instead of ________.
3 ________ instead of ________.
4 ________ instead of ________.

5 **Talk together: are all sea animals dangerous?**

People and the sea

How do people endanger the sea?

1 070 **Listen and point.**

1 plastic pollution

2 oil pollution

3 coral reef dying

4 ice melting

2 **Look at the pairs of photos. How do these pictures make you feel? Draw faces:** 🙂 😐 😣

3 **Talk about the pictures. Use the words below to help you.**

1 sea / clean / no plastic
2 sea / not clean / plastic
3 beach / clean
4 beach / dirty / lots of oil
5 coral reef / beautiful colours / fish
6 coral reef / white / no fish
7 ice / lots of
8 ice / smaller

In the first picture, the sea is clean and there isn't any plastic.

The sea in the second picture isn't clean. There's ....

4 071 **Listen, read and write the words in the correct spaces.**

Pollution Climate change

OUR SICK SEAS

Our seas are very important. Millions of sea creatures live in them. Sea plants make 50% of our oxygen and take 25% of our carbon dioxide. But our seas are in danger.

A ______________________

The world is getting hotter and the ice at the north and south poles is melting (becoming water). Because there is more water in the sea, there are more floods and many cities by the sea are in danger.

The sea is also getting hotter. This is bad for coral reefs because the hotter water is killing the coral. The coral is losing its beautiful colours and turning white. Sea creatures can't live in it any more and lots of starfish, seahorses and other fish are losing their homes.

B ______________________

Plastic pollution is a big problem for our oceans. There is lots of plastic rubbish, like bags and cups, in the water. Sea creatures sometimes eat the plastic. Lots of fish now have plastic inside them.

There are lots of big boats and ships on our oceans. They take things like clothes, televisions, food and people around the world. There is pollution from their oil in the water. Fish and coral reefs are dying from this pollution. Ships can also hit coral reefs.

5 Project **What can you do to stop climate change and sea pollution? Make a leaflet.**

Talk and find out

Where were we … ?

1 **Make a prediction.**

__________ classmates were at home on Saturday afternoon.

2 **Draw a table. Write in the names of the children from your group. Ask questions and write the answers in the table.**

Name	Where were you on Saturday afternoon?
James	at the theatre
Aruna	at home
Vee	in the swimming pool
Alice	at a friend's house

3 **Write a list of all the places. Tick ✓ the number of children and count them.**

Place	Number of children	Total
at the theatre	✓	1
at home	✓✓✓✓✓	5
at the cinema	✓✓	2
in a shop	✓✓✓	3
at a friend's house	✓✓✓✓	4
at a party	✓	1
in the garden	✓✓✓✓	4
in the swimming pool	✓✓	2

4 **Talk about your results.**

Was your prediction correct?

No, it wasn't. Five classmates were at home on Saturday afternoon.

Sea creatures

Writing tip

Making notes helps you to write.

1 Find information about a sea creature and make notes.

Animal: turtle

- What do they look like? brown, green, yellow, grey, four legs, hard shell
- Where do they live? in water (salt water and fresh water)
- How do they have their young? lay eggs in the sand on the beach, then go away, babies open egg, start to swim
- How long do they live? 40–70 years, but the oldest turtle is about 175 years old!
- Other interesting facts: turtles have got very good eyes, and they haven't got ears.

2 Find pictures and write about your sea creature.

TURTLES

I like turtles. They are beautiful. They are green, yellow, grey and brown. They live in the sea, rivers or lakes. They eat plants and small animals. Turtles lay eggs on beaches.

They put their eggs into the sand. The baby turtles swim. Turtles usually live for 40–70 years, but they can live up to 175 years.

6 Gadgets

1 072 **Listen and say the words. Then check with a friend.**

1 mobile phone
2 tablet
3 electric toothbrush
4 lift
5 torch
6 electric fan
7 walkie-talkie
8 laptop
9 games console

BIG QUESTION How are gadgets useful?

2 073 **Listen and answer.**

1 Where is the next letter?
2 What is £8?
3 What do they buy?
4 Who do they see?

3 **You are going on holiday. Decide what you want to buy.**

Let's buy an electric toothbrush.

Oh yes, and how about an electric fan?

1 074 **Listen and complete the table.**

£80 £99 big small

	price (£)	size
S2 20		
S5 30		

2 **Complete with *beautiful*, *cheaper* or *bigger*. Say the sentences.**

1 The S5 30 is ______________________ than the S2 20.

2 The S2 20 is ______________________ than the S5 30.

3 The S5 30 is more ______________________ than the S2 20.

3 075 **Watch, listen and say.**

Language focus

My phone's **smaller than** yours.

Your phone's **more beautiful than** mine.

My phone's **bigger than** yours.

It's **more expensive than** yours.

4 **Think of something in the classroom. Play the guessing game.**

Is it more expensive than the scissors?

Yes, it is.

Is it smaller than this scissors?

No, it isn't.

Is it the clock?

Yes, it is.

1 076 Listen and match the buttons to the gadgets. Then sing the song.

Look at my gadget.
It's really cool.
It's bigger than yours
More beautiful too.

Press the red button.
The torch comes on.
Press the blue button
It plays a song.

Look at my gadget.
It's really cool.
It's newer than yours
More expensive too.

Press the brown button.
The fan comes on.
Press the green button
And phone someone.

Look at my gadget.
It's really cool.
It's bigger than yours
More beautiful too.

2 Decide what happens when you press these buttons.

1 

2 

3 

3 Tell your friend about the buttons.

What happens when you press the purple button?

The walkie-talkie comes on. I use it to talk to my brother.

1 Read and number the pictures.

1 This is the fastest boat in the world. It can go at 511 km/h.

2 This is the most expensive watch in the world. It costs £45 million!

3 This is the tallest building in the world. It is 830m tall.

4 Is this the ugliest cat in the world? What do you think?

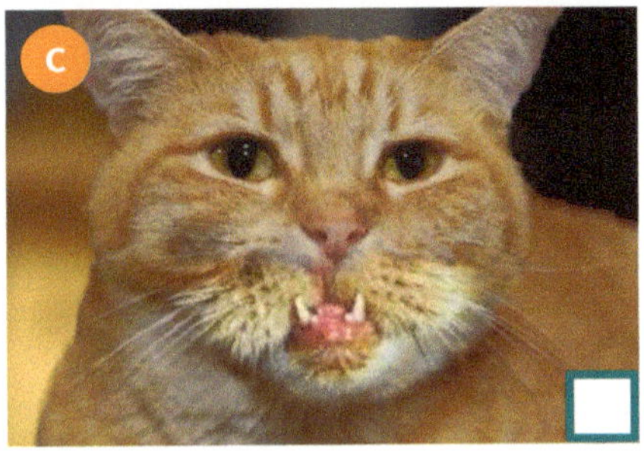

2 Put the words in order. Say the sentences.

1 is | the world. | This | the fastest | in | car

2 the most | house | expensive | the world. | in | is | This

3 Watch, listen and say.

078

Language focus

Our house is **the biggest** in the tree.
There's lots of room for Gina and me.
Our tree is **the tallest** in the wood.
Look at our tree. Life is good!
Our view is **the most beautiful** I know.
Careful Greg. Watch where you go!

4 Complete the sentences. Tell your friend.

1 ______________ is the tallest person in my family.

2 ______________ is the most difficult subject at school.

3 ______________ is the funniest person I know.

4 ______________ is the most exciting show on TV.

5 ______________ is the most beautiful place I know

My aunt is the tallest person in my family.

The cave

1 079 What do Horax and Zelda hear in the cave?

1

Lucy: The book says go to the caves. Here we are.
Ben: Somewhere down there is the next letter.

2

Ben: Stay here and watch for Horax and Zelda.
Lucy: OK. Have you got your walkie-talkie and torch?
Ben: Yes. I've got everything.

3

Ben: It's much darker down here. The torch was a good idea.
Lucy: Can you see the letter?
Ben: No, I can't.

4

Ben: Wow! What beautiful cave paintings! What's that? It's the letter *E*. *E* is the fifth letter in our puzzle.

5

Ben: Oh no. It's Zelda and Horax. I have to hide!

6

Horax: Where are those kids?
Ben: Lucy, I've got a problem. Horax and Zelda are here.
Lucy: Don't worry. I've got an idea.

Buster: Grrrrrr!
Zelda: What's that?
Horax: I don't know. I'm scared.
Zelda: Let's run!

Ben: Great idea, Lucy!
Lucy: Well done, Buster. You're the cleverest dog in the world.

2 Write a quiz for the story. Here are the answers.

1 Go to the caves. ______________________________?
2 Ben. ______________________________?
3 Lucy. ______________________________?
4 The letter *E*. ______________________________?
5 Behind a rock. ______________________________?
6 Buster. ______________________________?

Phonics

3 Find who says ... What beautiful cave paintings!

4 080 Listen and say.

Irene uses her phone to find the limes for her cake.

1 Read and circle.

1 **Assistant:** Can I help you?
Dan:
a No, I can't help you.
b Yes, I'd like to buy a torch.
c Yes, I've got a torch.

2 **Dan:** How much is this torch?
Assistant:
a It's £20.
b It's 20 kg.
c It's 20 cm.

3 **Dan:** Have you got a cheaper one?
Assistant:
a Yes, this one is £12.
b It's cheaper than the walkie-talkie.
c It's the most expensive.

4 **Dan:** I'd like to buy it.
Assistant:
a Come back tomorrow.
b I've got an idea.
c Yes, of course.

5 **Dan:** Goodbye!
Assistant:
a Goodbye and thank you!
b Yes, please.
c Oh dear!

2 Look at the pictures and talk about the differences.

The fan in A is cheaper than the fan in B.

1 Look carefully. Close your books and say.

There are some sunglasses.

2 081 Listen and tick ☑ the gadgets that Ana has got.

3 082 Listen again and complete the sentences.

1 The sunglasses are also a ______________.
2 The fan is also a ______________.
3 The watch is also a ______________.
4 Ana uses the electric toothbrush to ______________ her ______________.

4 Choose a spy gadget. Draw a picture and write sentences about it.

This is a spy tablet.
It is also a skateboard.
You can use it to escape!

CAVE PAINTINGS

What materials did cave artists use in the past?

Super fact!

The oldest cave painting in the world is in Indonesia. It's more than 40,000 years old. The painting is of a kind of cow.

1 083 Listen and point.

charcoal

rock powder

twig

lamp

cave ceiling

2 Read and answer the questions.

Long ago, cave artists liked painting pictures on the walls and ceilings of their caves. They used small lamps to see their paintings because it was very dark inside the caves. We can see very old paintings of animals and birds in some caves today and sometimes the paintings tell a story.

The colours in cave paintings are usually black, red, yellow, orange and brown. The colour black comes from charcoal. Artists used this to draw the lines of the animals. The colours red, yellow, orange and brown come from rock powder. Artists mixed the powder with water to make paint and they used their fingers and small twigs from trees to put the paint on the cave walls.

1 Where were the cave paintings?
2 What was it like in the caves?
3 What did they paint?
4 Do the paintings tell a story?
5 What colours are in the cave paintings?
6 What did they use to put the paint on the walls?

3 What would you paint on a cave wall today?

Places: My house ______ People: ______
Animals: ______ Gadgets: ______

4 Look, read and match.

Today, artists use pencils, brushes and paints but there weren't any of these things for cave artists.

Things artists use today

1

2

3

4
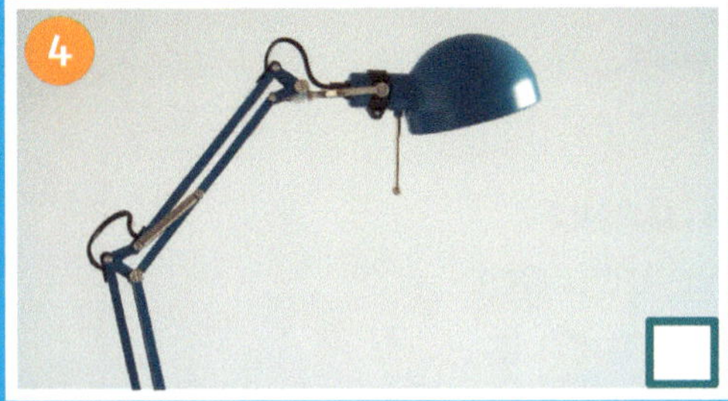

Things cave artists used

a

b

c

d

5 084 Listen and check.

6 Project Make a cave painting from life today. Write about your picture.

This is a cave painting of my house.
That's me at my bedroom window.

Talk and find out

Go shopping

1 **Choose a role card. Read and plan.**

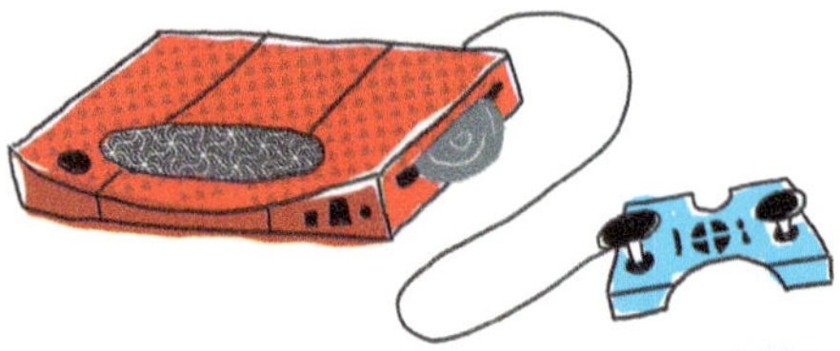

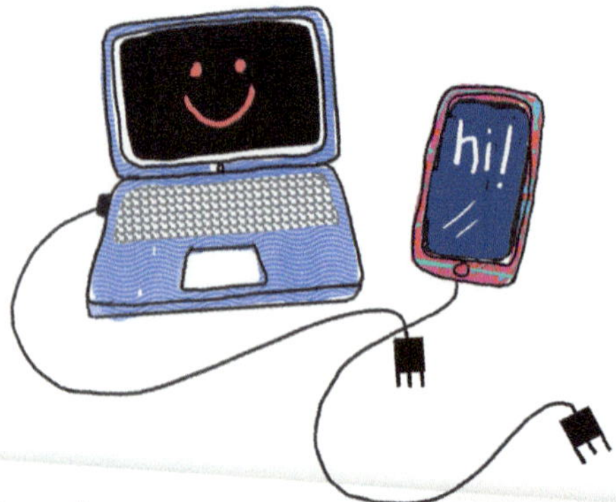

Student A

You are in a shop. Choose three things you want to buy:

- a torch
- a walkie-talkie
- a tablet
- a games console
- an electric toothbrush
- a laptop

You have £100 to spend. Talk to the shop assistant and see what you can buy.

Student B

You are a shop assistant. Find out the prices from your teacher and write them:

- a torch £ ______
- a walkie-talkie £ ______
- a tablet £ ______
- a games console £ ______
- an electric toothbrush £ ______
- a laptop £ ______

Talk to the customer and help him/her buy some gadgets.

Useful language

Assistant	**Customer**
Good morning/afternoon.	Have you got … ?
Can I help you?	How much is … ?
Yes, we have. / No, we haven't.	All right, so can I buy it?
It's … pound(s).	Thank you.
Of course!	

2 **Act out your play.**

Good morning. Can I help you?

Yes, have you got any torches?

Yes, we have.

Think and write

My gadgets

1 Think of some toys or gadgets you have. Write words about them in a table.

Gadget	Got it when? Who from?	Looks?	Other facts?
bike	birthday present, from my parents	red and black, bigger than old bike, very beautiful	cycle to lots of places, sometimes to visit grandmother
mobile phone	got with money from grandfather	small, silver, looks cool	listen to music before going to bed, love it!
camera	…	…	…

2 Tell your friend about your favourite gadget.

It's my bike.
I got it for my last birthday.
I got it from my parents.

3 Write about your favourite gadget.

My favourite gadget is my bike.

It was my birthday present from my parents. My old bike was very small. This bike is bigger.

It's red and black. It's the most beautiful bike in the world.

I love my bike. I cycle to lots of places on it. I sometimes ride my bike to visit my grandmother at the weekend.

Writing tip

Read your writing slowly to check your spelling.

7 In the hospital

1 085 **Listen and say the words. Then check with a friend.**

1 earache
2 headache
3 cold
4 toothache
5 stomach-ache
6 cough
7 doctor
8 nurse

BIG QUESTION What keeps us healthy?

2 086 **Listen and correct the sentences.**

1 The message says Lucy's dad is in the hospital.
2 Grandpa's room is downstairs.
3 The nurse shows them where the room is.
4 Ben and Lucy walk up the stairs.

3 **Play the mime game.**

What's the matter with me?

You've got stomach-ache.

That's right.

1 087 Listen and number the pictures.

2 Look at Activity 1 again and write the correct words. Say the sentences.

play → played shout → shouted land → landed jump → jumped

1 Yesterday, Harry __________ basketball.

2 He __________ up high.

3 He __________ on the floor.

4 'Ouch!' he __________.

3 088 Watch, listen and say.

Language focus

Greg was in the garden and **looked** up at the tree.
Greg **shouted**, 'Gina, come and climb with me!'
Gina **smiled** and said, 'OK. That looks fun!'
They **climbed**, then they **rested** in the hot, hot sun.
They **jumped** down from the tree, down into the pool.
They **landed** in the water – it was nice and cool.

4 Change the words to talk about yesterday. Ask and answer.

watch _ed_ listen ____ to visit ____ phone ____ play ____ walk ____

What happened yesterday?

I watched a film and played tennis. And you?

1 089 Listen and match. Then sing the song.

The doctor always tells me,
'An apple's good for you.'
Well listen to my story.
It isn't always true.

I was in the kitchen,
There was apple cake.
I swallowed it but it was big,
I've got stomach-ache.

It's not true! It's not true!
It isn't always true
What the doctor tells me,
isn't always true!

I was at the apple farm,
I looked up at a snake!
I walked into an apple tree
My head now really aches.

It's not true! It's not true! …

I was at the market
With my family,
I took a box of apples but
They landed on my knee.

It's not true! It's not true! …

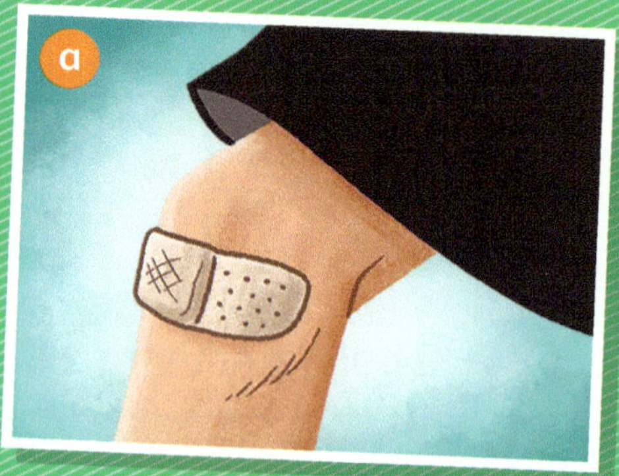

2 Look at the pictures above. Say what happened to the girl.

First she ate a big apple cake. Then she …

3 Work with a partner. Close your eyes. Imagine what happened to the girl the next day.

The next day, she …
There was / were …
She looked and …
…

1 Look, read and complete the story.

Yesterday I woke up early. I felt terrible. I had a bad (1) __________.
I went to see the (2) __________ with my dad.
She gave me some (3) __________.
'No (4) __________ today,' she said.
'Great,' I said. 'No problem,' said my dad. 'Today is Saturday.'

2 Look at Activity 1 again. Write the past form of the verbs.

1 wake up → ________ up
2 feel → __________
3 have → __________
4 go → __________
5 give → __________
6 say → __________

3 091 Watch, listen and say.

Language focus

Greg **woke up** about half past eight.
He **felt** bad. He **had** a stomach-ache.
'You **had** too many flies,' Mum **said**.
She **gave** him a drink and he **went** back to bed.

4 Use the pictures to write a story about Millie.

1 092 Who saves Ben and Lucy?

Doctor: Here we are. Room 209. Go right in, kids. I'll see you and your grandfather later.

Ben: Thanks so much, Doctor.

Lucy: There's no answer. Your grandpa is sleeping.

Ben: OK, let's go in quietly.

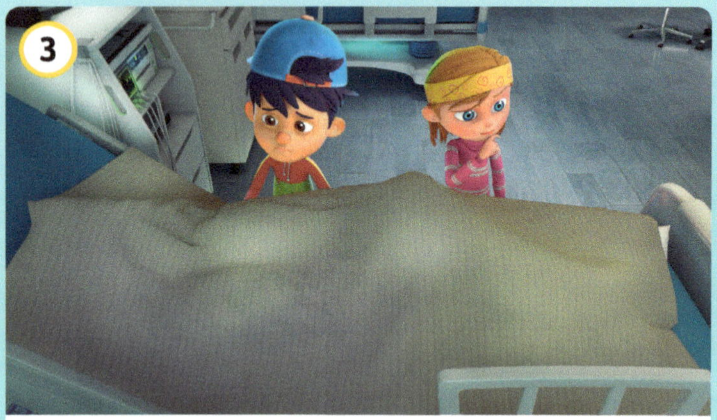

Ben: Grandpa? Are you all right? I got a text message. It said you're in hospital.

Lucy: Something isn't right.

Ben: Oh no. It's a trap!

Lucy: Someone played a trick on us!

Horax: Ha ha! It's so nice of you to visit me in hospital. Welcome, children!

Ben: What do you want from us, Horax? Leave us alone!

Horax: You know what I want. I want the book, and I want the letters.

Lucy: No way! The book is ours. We found it in the castle!

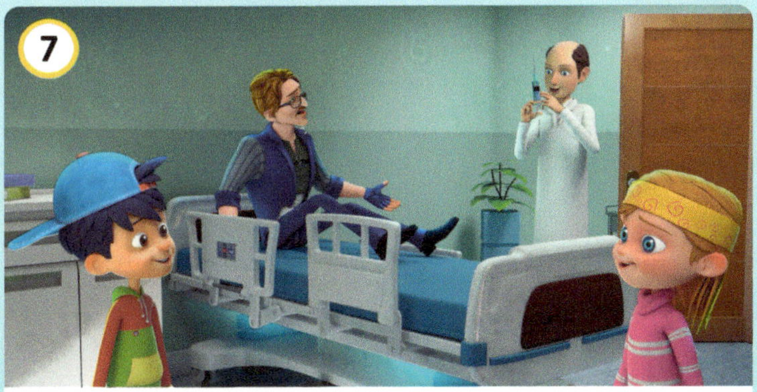

Doctor: Please go outside for a moment, kids. Your grandfather needs an injection.
Horax: Well, I'm ... I mean ... I'm not ...
Doctor: Just lie down on the bed, please.

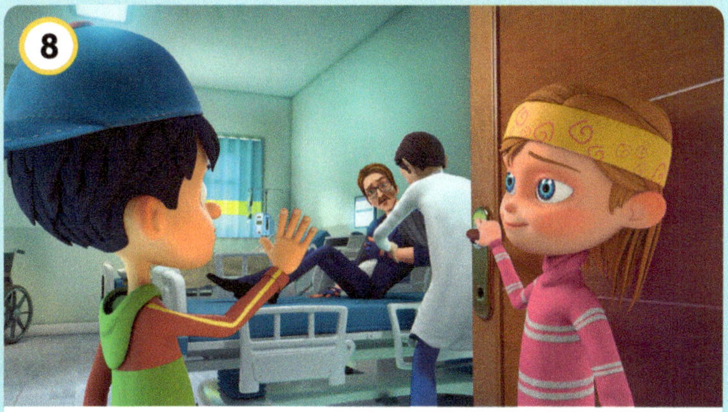

Lucy: Thanks, Doctor. We have to go now!
Ben: Bye-bye, Grandpa. Hope you get better soon!
Horax: Don't go! Wait! I want to ...

2 Read and draw lines to make sentences.

1 Ben got
2 It said, 'Go to the hospital,'
3 They found Horax
4 Horax wanted
5 At that moment
6 Lucy and Ben said, 'Bye-bye'

a and not Ben's grandfather there!
b the book and the letters.
c the doctor came in.
d a text message.
e and went out of the room.
f but it was a trick.

Phonics

3 Find who says ...

Someone played a trick on us!

4 093 Listen and say.

Mike hiked – he liked it.

Kate skated – she hated it.

1 **Read the story quickly. Write the answers.**

1 What is the girl's name?

2 What was the girl's problem?

3 What's the dog's name?

2 094 **Read and listen. Check your answers.**

A new best friend

Emma Woodward was 11 years old. She liked swimming and riding her bike. But one day Emma woke up with a headache. It got worse and worse and Emma felt very ill. Her parents took her to a hospital and she saw the doctor straight away. Emma couldn't walk or stand up. The doctor looked at her very carefully. 'There's a problem with Emma's head, she needs an operation straight away.'

After the operation Emma was asleep. When she woke up she had to stay in bed for a long time. She couldn't remember how to do anything. The doctor said 'Emma's legs are not strong. She needs to use a wheelchair. When she's not in the wheelchair, she needs crutches.' Emma was very tired and didn't try to walk. 'I can't do it!' she said. Her parents were worried. 'What can we do? How can we help Emma?' they asked.

One day Emma's mum heard about the Helper Dog Project. The project had dogs to help people with many different kinds of problems.

The next day, they went to see the Helper Dog Project. Emma was on her crutches. She went from the car to the building. She was very tired. She sat in a chair. Then one of the dogs came over. His name was Jasper, and he was the biggest dog in the room. He looked at Emma. Then he put his paw on Emma's leg. Emma knew Jasper was her new best friend.

The family took Jasper home and with his help Emma slowly learned to walk again. She put one hand on Jasper and used her other hand to hold a crutch. It was difficult but every day, Emma walked a little more. Soon she started to walk with no crutches using Jasper to help her.

These days Emma and Jasper are always together. Jasper even goes to school with Emma. When she is reading or writing, Jasper sleeps under her desk.

Last week there was a surprise for Jasper and Emma. A magazine gave Jasper a big prize – The Best Animal of the Year! The next day, the story about the little girl and the big dog was in all the newspapers.

'Look!' Emma said to Jasper. 'You are now the most famous dog in the world!'

Jasper looked at Emma. Then he put his paw on her leg. She remembered the first time she saw Jasper and smiled.

3 Put the story in order.

- ☐ Emma's mum and dad went to the Helper Dog Project with Emma.
- ☐ Emma liked the biggest dog, Jasper, a lot.
- ☐ Emma Woodward had a bad headache.
- ☐ Her parents took her to hospital.
- ☐ Jasper got a big prize, The Best Animal of the Year!
- ☐ The doctor said, 'You have to sit in a wheelchair or use crutches.'
- ☐ With Jasper's help, Emma learnt to walk again.

4 095 Listen to a summary of the story. Write the four differences.

In the summary we have …

1 stomach-ache instead of a headache.
2 ______ instead of ______.
3 ______ instead of ______.
4 ______ instead of ______.

KEEPING HEALTHY

How can we keep healthy?

1 096 Listen and point.

Super fact!

It's OK to eat unhealthy food sometimes. Just don't *always* eat it.

1 exercise

2 healthy food

3 unhealthy food

4 sleep

5 rest

6 fresh air

2 Read about healthy food, exercise, fresh air and rest. Then write.

Eating healthy food, doing exercise, and getting fresh air and rest help us to keep healthy.

healthy food

Try to eat some fruit and vegetables and some bread, pasta or rice every day. Don't eat a lot of the same food, like chips, pizza or ice cream.

rest

Rest is also very important. You can rest by doing things like reading a book. The best way to rest is to sleep. That's why it's important to get a good sleep every night.

fresh air

Go outside and get some fresh air! You can cycle to school or to a friend's house.

exercise

Try and exercise often to stay strong. Swimming, cycling and doing sports make us healthy. You can exercise with friends.

1 Write four examples of healthy food.
2 Write four ways of getting exercise.
3 Write two outdoor activities.
4 Write two ways of getting rest.

3 Put these activities into the correct column.

swimming   playing computer games for four hours   always going to bed very late
always eating ice cream for lunch   walking to school   laughing with friends

HEALTHY	UNHEALTHY

4 Look at the pictures. Write *healthy* or *unhealthy*.

a

____

b

____

c

____

d

____

5 Match the sentences with the pictures in Activity 4.

1 These are bad for the teeth. ☐
2 It gets me outdoors. ☐
3 Sometimes it makes my eyes ache. ☐
4 I always make healthy food. ☐

6 Tell your partner about two things you do to keep healthy.

I play football to keep healthy.

7 Project Make a storyboard or slide presentation to show how you keep healthy. Write some words in each box or on each slide.

I play tennis to keep healthy. I usually play tennis with my friends on Saturdays.

Talk and find out

At the doctor's

1 Choose a role card. Read and plan.

Student A

You are the doctor. A patient is coming to see you.

- Ask what the problem is.
- Ask what happened.
- Check the problem.
- Say what the patient has to do.

Student B

You are the patient.

- You have a pain. Decide what the problem is.
- Tell the doctor what happened.
- Tell the doctor where you have the pain.
- Tell the doctor what you want to do tomorrow.

Useful language

Doctor

What's the matter?
What happened?
Let me see.
You have to take some medicine / drink lots of water / stay in bed …
No problem. / No, you can't. You have to …

Patient

I've got a pain in my …
I kicked … / jumped … / landed on …
Ouch!
Yes, of course. I want to play … / go … tomorrow. Is that OK?

2 Act out your play.

Good morning, Doctor.

Good morning.
What's the matter?

Write a story

Writing tip

Write stories in the past tense. Remember to check your verbs!

1 Think of a story. It can be a true story or a story you imagine. Use the questions to help you.

Who is the story about?	Tom, 12 years old, good swimmer
When?	3 weeks ago, Sunday
What was the weather like?	very sunny, hot
What happened?	swimming, jumped into pool, problem, not a lot of water, hurt his head, hospital, 3 weeks

2 Plan and write notes about your story. Draw pictures.

 Tom – great swimmer.	Sunday, three weeks ago – sunny and very hot. 	Tom jumped into the pool. 
 Not a lot of water.	Tom hurt his head. 	Tom was in hospital for 3 weeks. 

3 Draw and write a story.

Tom loved swimming. He was very good at it.

One Sunday, it was very hot and Tom wanted to swim. He jumped into the pool, but there was not much water in it.

8 Around the world

1 Listen and say the words. Then check with a friend. (097)

1 Egypt
2 Argentina
3 India
4 Australia
5 Mexico
6 Brazil
7 Chile
8 Spain
9 China
10 Turkey

BIG QUESTION What wonders of the world are there?

Stay at home but travel far.
The missing letter is where you are.

2 (098) Listen and answer.

1 Who had the idea to go to the park?
2 How much is one ticket?
3 How much change does Lucy get?
4 Where does Ben want to go first and why?

3 Play the flag game.

It's yellow and green.

Egypt.

Wrong. One point for me.

1 (099) Listen and tick ☑ the pictures.

1 Sara went …

a 

b 

2 She saw …

a 

b 

3 She ate …

a 

b 

2 Where do the words go? Say the sentences.

1 I went to the zoo with my mum but dad go with us. (didn't)

2 We went to a pizza restaurant but I have a pizza. (didn't)

3 (100) Watch, listen and say.

Language focus

I went to the sea, but I **didn't have** fun.

The beach was cold, so I **didn't stay** for long.

4 Play the chain game.

We went on holiday but we didn't eat ice cream.

We went on holiday but we didn't eat ice cream and we didn't go in the sea.

1 101 **Listen and match the countries with the pictures. Then sing the song.**

All the wonders in the world
I didn't see a single one.
All the wonders in the world
I was having too much fun.

I went to China
But I didn't see the wall.
In India
I didn't see the Taj Mahal.

All the wonders in the world ...

I went to Egypt
But I didn't see the Sphinx.
I went to Spain
But I didn't see a lynx.

All the wonders in the world ...

I went to Australia
But I didn't see the sun.
And in Brazil
I didn't see the Amazon.

All the wonders in the world ...

1 
China

2 
India

3 
Egypt

4 
Spain

5 
Brazil

a 
The Sphinx

b 
The Amazon

c 
A lynx

d 
The Great Wall

e 
The Taj Mahal

2 **Make a list of wonders in your country.**

3 **Compare with a friend.**

I think the national museum is a wonder.

I think the panda is a wonder.

1 103 **Match the questions with the answers. Then listen and check.**

1 Did you have fun in New York?
2 Who did you go with?
3 How long did you stay there?
4 Where did you stay?
5 Did you go to the Guggenheim Museum?
6 Did you send me a postcard?

☐ No, I didn't. We didn't have time.
☐ For a week.
☐ Yes, I did. It was great.
☐ Sorry! I forgot.
☐ Mum and Dad and Bobby.
☐ In a hotel near Central Park.

2 **Put the words in order. Say the sentences.**

1 have you Did holiday? a good
2 did there? you Who see
3 How get there? you did
4 get you When home? did back

3 104 **Watch, listen and say.**

Language focus

Did you **go** to Spain, Greg?
Yes, I **did**.
Did you **go** by plane, Greg?
No, I **didn't**.

When **did** you **get** home, Greg?
Yesterday.

4 **Ask your friend questions about their last holiday.**

Where … ?
… have fun?
How long … ?
How did you … ?
Who … go with?

1 105 **What are Ben and Lucy doing when Horax takes the book?**

Lucy: What a great football stadium!
Ben: Yes, I'd love to go to Rio de Janeiro!
Lucy: Where next?
Ben: You choose.

Ben: The Great Wall of China. It's amazing!
Lucy: Yes, it is. But where are these letters? Have you got any idea, Ben?
Ben: Not yet, but let's keep looking.

Ben: What's this?
Lucy: It's the opera house in Sydney, in Australia.

Ben: Hey, look. It's Mr Williams.
Mr Williams: Hi, kids. What are you doing here?
Lucy: Hello! We're learning about the world.
Mr Williams: Well, have a good day.

Lucy: The pyramids and the Sphinx. Cool!
Ben: But still no letters. Where can they be?

Ben: I'm hungry. I didn't have a very big breakfast this morning.
Lucy: I'm glad we made these sandwiches.

 Value: showing interest in other cultures; reading for pleasure

Lucy: The book! It isn't here!
Ben: What happened? Did you drop it?
Lucy: I'm not sure. What can we do?

Ben: We have to go and look for the book.
Lucy: Maybe not! I can see the missing letters!
Ben: What? The *I*, *I* and *A*?
Lucy: No, the *N* and *D*!

2 Look, read and answer.

In which picture do they visit … ?

a ☐ b ☐ c ☐ d ☐ e ☐

Phonics

3 Find who says …

It's the opera house in Sydney, in Australia.

4 106 Listen and say.

Silly Milly made a pyramid of jelly at the gym.

1 107 Listen and draw lines.

Daisy Mary Vicky Fred

Peter Paul Jack

2 Read and write the words.

The Great Pyramid of Khufu **(1)** ________ in Giza, near Cairo. The ancient Egyptians built **(2)** ________ 5,000 years ago. It is about 140 metres high. It was the **(3)** ________ building in the world for a very long time. In **(4)** ________ of the pyramid is the Sphinx. It has the body of a lion and the head **(5)** ________ a man.

1	**a** are	**b** is	**c** am
2	**a** it	**b** them	**c** him
3	**a** tall	**b** taller	**c** tallest
4	**a** behind	**b** next	**c** front
5	**a** by	**b** on	**c** of

1 Read and talk about the questions.

You win a competition. The prize is a trip around the world.

You have one year and you can visit six countries.

You can take one person with you.

- Which countries do you want to visit?
- How do you want to travel?
- What do you want to see?
- Who do you want to take with you?

2 Read Megan's travel blog. Match each day with a photo.

Megan's travel blog

a

Day ________

b

Day ________

c

Day ________

Day 34

Today we saw an amazing waterfall. It's called the Iguazu falls. There was so much water! And it was really loud. We also visited three countries in one day. The Iguazu falls are in Brazil and Argentina (and close to Paraguay too!)

Day 78

Paris is the most beautiful city in the world, and today I saw the Eiffel tower. I took loads of photos. We didn't go up because we were very tired but we're going to tomorrow. We already have our tickets.

Day 187

This is our second day on Safari. The animals are amazing. Yesterday we saw elephants, giraffes and lots of monkeys. Today we saw lions! They were beautiful. I was a little bit scared and I was happy when we got back to camp.

3 Read again and correct the sentences.

1 The Iguazu falls are in Paraguay and Brazil.

2 Megan has tickets to visit the Louvre museum in Paris.

3 Megan thought the elephants were beautiful but scary.

Today we landed in Sydney, Australia. We were very tired but we were also very excited.

4 Write about one day on your around-the-world trip.

Wonders of the world

What are some of the natural wonders of the world?

Super fact!

You can see the Great Barrier Reef from space.

1 108 Listen and point.

2 **Read, look at the map and write the continents.**

1 Lots of interesting animals, like pink snakes, live in the Grand Canyon. It's in ______________.

2 The Harbour of Rio de Janeiro is in ______________. There are more than 80 kilometres of beaches next to it.

3 The Northern Lights are usually green, red or pink. You can see them in ______________.

4 Paricutin Volcano is in ______________. It's 3,170 metres high.

5 Mount Everest is more than 60 million years old. It's in ______________.

6 The Great Barrier Reef is in ______________. More than 1,500 kinds of fish live there.

7 Victoria Falls is in ______________. The water comes from the Zambezi river.

3 **What's the nearest natural wonder of the world to you?**

The nearest wonder of the world to me is … It's in …

4 (109) Match the facts with the man-made wonders. Listen and check.

There are also wonders of the world made by people. We can call them 'man-made' wonders. Here are some of them.

a

The Great Pyramid of Giza, Egypt

b

The Great Wall, China

c

The Taj Mahal, India

1 There are more than 2.3 million stones in it. ☐
2 The Emperor Shah Jahan built it to remember his wife. ☐
3 Many people think you can see it from the moon but that's not true. ☐
4 It's 170 metres tall. ☐
5 They built it in 20 years. ☐
6 It's the longest wall in the world. ☐

5 Talk about a natural or man-made wonder of the world. Use the words to help you.

beautiful old big interesting

Which wonder of the world do you want to see?

I want to see the Great Barrier Reef. It's very beautiful and very big.

6 Project Make a poster with your two favourite wonders of the world. Write a few sentences and a question about each wonder.

My favourite wonders of the world

This is the Great Pyramid of Giza. It is in Egypt. How tall is it?

This is the Paricutin Volcano. It is the youngest volcano in America. How old is it?

Talk and find out

What did we do on our holidays?

1 **Make a prediction.**

I predict that __________ classmates visited the beach on holiday.

2 **Ask questions.**

What did you do on holiday?

- Visit relatives?
- Go to the beach?
- Go to the mountains?
- Visit a museum?
- Go camping?
- Go hiking?
- Relax?

3 **Write the information on the board.**

visit relatives – 6

go to the beach – 9

go to the mountains – 0

4 **Make a chart and talk about the results.**

Was your prediction correct?

Yes, it was. 9 classmates visited the beach on holiday.

Write about a country

1 Choose a country. Find information about the country. Make notes.

Writing tip

Remember that names of cities and countries always start with a capital letter.

country: Spain
where: Europe
cities: Madrid, Barcelona, Málaga
famous for: sea, mountains, sun, Picasso, football

2 Make an information tree about your country.

3 Find pictures and write about your country.

Spain is in Europe. The capital city is Madrid. It is in the middle of the country. Spain has got two great football teams: Real Madrid and Barcelona. Barcelona is another famous city in Spain. It's by the sea. It's got lots of amazing buildings. There are beautiful mountains in the north of Spain, next to France. Picasso was a famous painter from Spain. One day I would like to go to Spain for a holiday.

9 Holiday plans

1 **110** **Listen and say the words. Then check with a friend.**

1 thunderstorm
2 cloud(y)
3 lightning
4 rain(y)
5 wind(y)
6 umbrella
7 raincoat
8 fog(gy)
9 boots

BIG QUESTION **How are holidays different?**

2 **111** **Listen and correct the sentences.**

1 Ben is scared of thunderstorms.
2 They are a long way from the castle.
3 Ben and Lucy have got the book.
4 Ben and Lucy have to find two more letters.

3 **Play the mime game.**

I think you're holding an umbrella.

Yes, I am!

1 (112) Listen and draw lines.

Monday Tuesday Wednesday Thursday Friday

sunny

foggy

rainy

cloudy

windy

2 Where do the words go? Say the sentences.

1 I'm be in the garden all day. (going to)
2 It's not going rainy on Tuesday. (to be)

3 (113) Watch, listen and say.

Language focus

It'**s not going to be** sunny on Monday,
It'**s not going to be** sunny on Wednesday,
And it'**s going to be** rainy on Saturday.

Well, I'**m going to play** outside every day!
Do you want to come out, too?
Yes, I do! I'**m going to play** with you.

4 Play the weather game.

1 114 Listen and number the pictures. Then sing the song.

Holiday!
Enjoy your time away!
Holiday!
Let's shout Hooray! Hooray!

I'm going to stay in bed
And read my favourite book.
I'm going to see my aunt.
She's going to teach me how to cook.

Holiday! ...

I'm going to travel far away.
I'm going to have some fun.
Then I'm going to rest at home.
And lie down in the sun.

Holiday! ...

After our holiday, we're going to be at school.
We're going to see our friends again,
Being with friends is cool!

Holiday! ...

2 Talk about your holidays.

I'm going to read my favourite book.

I'm not going to visit my aunt.

3 Draw a Venn diagram.

1 116 Listen, read and write the names under the pictures.

Mrs Beal: Lily, what are you going to do in your holiday?

Lily: Nothing much. I'm going to read lots of books.

Mrs Beal: Oliver and James, what are you going to do?

James: We're going to stay at home and play all our computer games.

Mrs Beal: Ruby, what are you going to do in your holiday?

Ruby: I'm going to Mexico with my mum and dad. I'm going to swim all day.

Mrs Beal: Dylan, what are you going to do in your holiday?

Dylan: I'm going to play lots of football and tennis.

2 Use the words to make *be going to* questions. Say the sentences.

1 Tim / what / you / do in your holidays?

2 Mum / what / we / do in our holidays?

3 117 Watch, listen and say.

Language focus

Are you **going to climb** some trees?
Yes, I am.

Are you **going to eat** some sweets?
No, I'm not.

Are you **going to go** away?
No, I'm not. I'm going to stay.

4 Look and play the holiday game.

Are you going to listen to music?

Yes, I am.

1 118 **Where are Ben and Lucy going to take the golden statue?**

Lucy: Look. It's Horax and Zelda. What are they doing?

Ben: I don't know, but they've got our book.

Lucy: Let's hide and find out.

Horax: There's a message with a missing word. We need the letters!

Ben: Atchoo!

Zelda: What was that?

Horax: How kind of you to visit us!

Zelda: Now, give us the letters.

Ben: OK, they're *N F D I S E R*.

Horax: Hmm. So, it's a kind of puzzle.

Zelda: Go away, stupid dog!

Lucy: No! It can't be! You're Mr Williams!

Horax: Yes, now you know. But it doesn't matter. I've got what I need.

Horax: These letters are a puzzle.

Zelda: Yes. I think they make a word.

Horax: Look! The letters make the word *finders*. Let's write it!

Horax: What? The word has to be *finders*! That's what we are – finders!

Zelda: It's wrong, you fool. Why do you always get things wrong?

7

Lucy: The word is *friends* not *finders*. Only true friends can go in here. Come on, Ben!

8

Ben: Wow! It's beautiful!

Lucy: It's amazing! Let's take it to the museum. That's where it belongs.

Ben: What a perfect end to our adventure!

2 **Use the code to find out what the statue says.**

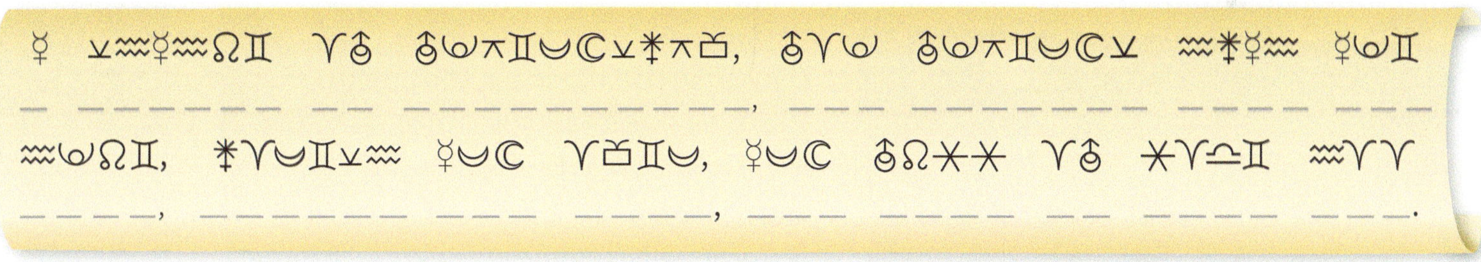

Phonics

3 **Find who says …** What a p**er**fect end to our adventure!

4 119 **Listen and say.**

There are c**ir**cles of p**ur**ple b**ir**ds wearing their holiday sh**ir**ts.

1 **Read the story quickly. Write the answers.**

1 Where did Liam and his family go on holiday?

2 What was the weather like?

3 Why was it a very different holiday?

2 120 **Read and listen. Check your answers.**

A very different holiday

Liam was very excited. 'We're going to Florida for two weeks. We're going to swim a lot and we're going to see lots of beautiful fish. It's going to be fantastic!' he said. His mum and dad were excited about the holiday too. 'We can go for boat rides!' said Dad. 'We can relax and have a lot of fun!' said Mum.

They arrived in Florida in the afternoon. The hotel was beautiful, and close to the sea. Their rooms had big windows. Liam loved looking at the sea and the boats. 'Tomorrow I'm going to swim in the sea!' he said.

That evening, they sat on the balcony for more than an hour. It was dark and there were lots of stars. They listened to the sea. 'This is going to be a great holiday,' said Liam.

In the middle of the night Liam woke up. 'What's that noise?' he thought. He looked outside and saw a big thunderstorm. Liam felt a little scared. 'We're OK here, Liam,' said Dad. 'But the weather isn't looking good. Let's switch on the TV.'

'There's going to be a lot of rain in Florida for the next fourteen days,' said the man on TV. 'There are going to be thunderstorms with strong winds and lots of lightning. It's going to be much colder than normal too.'

Liam looked at his dad. Then he looked at his mum. They were both quiet. 'That can't be true! It's our holiday. We can't swim or see fish in the rain! It's going to be boring,' Liam said.

'The most important thing is that we're on holiday,' answered Mum. 'We can have fun in our room. We can read, play games and listen to music. We don't need sun to have a good time!'

Two weeks later, their holiday was finished. 'I don't want to go home, Mum,' Liam said. 'We didn't go swimming or see any beautiful fish, and we didn't go on a boat ride. But it was a beautiful holiday!'

'I agree,' Mum said. 'Let's finish packing later. Let's play another game first!' Dad went to get their games box. 'Hooray!' shouted Liam.

3 Put the story in order.

- ☐ Liam had a good time inside with his mum and dad.
- ☐ Liam woke up because of a noisy thunderstorm.
- ☐ Liam and his mum and dad went to Florida for a holiday.
- ☐ Liam loved his holiday so much he didn't want to go home.
- ☐ Liam's dad switched on the TV.
- ☐ The man on TV said, 'There's going to be rain for fourteen days!'
- ☐ Liam didn't like that. 'It's going to be boring!' he thought.

4 121 Listen to a summary of the story. Write the four differences.

In the summary we have …

1 Italy instead of Florida.

2 ______ instead of ______.

3 ______ instead of ______.

4 ______ instead of ______.

HOLIDAYS IN THE PAST

Super fact!

100 years ago, people didn't go on holiday by plane. They went by train or boat.

How were seaside holidays different 100 years ago?

1 122 Listen and point.

1 puppet show

2 steam train

3 crowded beach

4 swimming boots

5 donkey ride

6 picnic basket

7 ice cream cart

2 Read about beach holidays 100 years ago.

100 years ago, many families went on holiday to the seaside by steam train. The beaches were very crowded with people. People wore special swimming boots in the water but they didn't wear sunglasses. Children played in the sand and in the water. They liked watching puppet shows and going on donkey rides. Many families had picnic baskets with sandwiches, fruit and lemonade in them for lunch. Sometimes a cart came to the beach with ice cream for people to buy.

3 Match the sentences with the words.

1 This was crowded.
2 Many families went to the seaside on this.
3 People went swimming in these.
4 Children liked watching this.
5 This had sandwiches in it.
6 Children liked riding this.
7 This sometimes came to the beach.

a an ice cream cart
b a picnic basket
c a donkey
d a steam train
e the beach
f a puppet show
g swimming boots

4 What's different about a beach holiday now and a beach holiday 100 years ago? Find two differences. Find two things that are the same.

> 100 years ago, people went to the seaside by steam train. Now, they go by car.

5 Holidays now or holidays 50 years ago? Look at the pictures and write the numbers in the table.

Sleeping

1

2

Cooking

3

4

Playing

5

6

Camping 50 years ago	Camping now

6 Circle the pictures that you think could be in both groups.

7 Project Make a storyboard about a holiday when you were younger.

We went to the lake. We went by steam train.

We played with our ball and went swimming.

For lunch we had a picnic and some ice cream.

We went for a long walk after lunch.

We felt happy.

Talk and find out

Holiday time

1 Work in pairs. Read the role card.

You are going on holiday with a friend. Decide:

- Where you are going.
- How long you are going for.
- How you are going to get there.
- What you are going to do there.

Useful language

Student A	Student B
I'd like to go to …	I don't want to go to …
OK. What about … ?	Yes, that's a great idea.
We could …	Fantastic!
Do you like … ?	Yes, I do. / No, I don't.

2 Plan your holiday.

3 Work in groups.

Think and write

Imagine a holiday

1 Make a mind map about holidays.

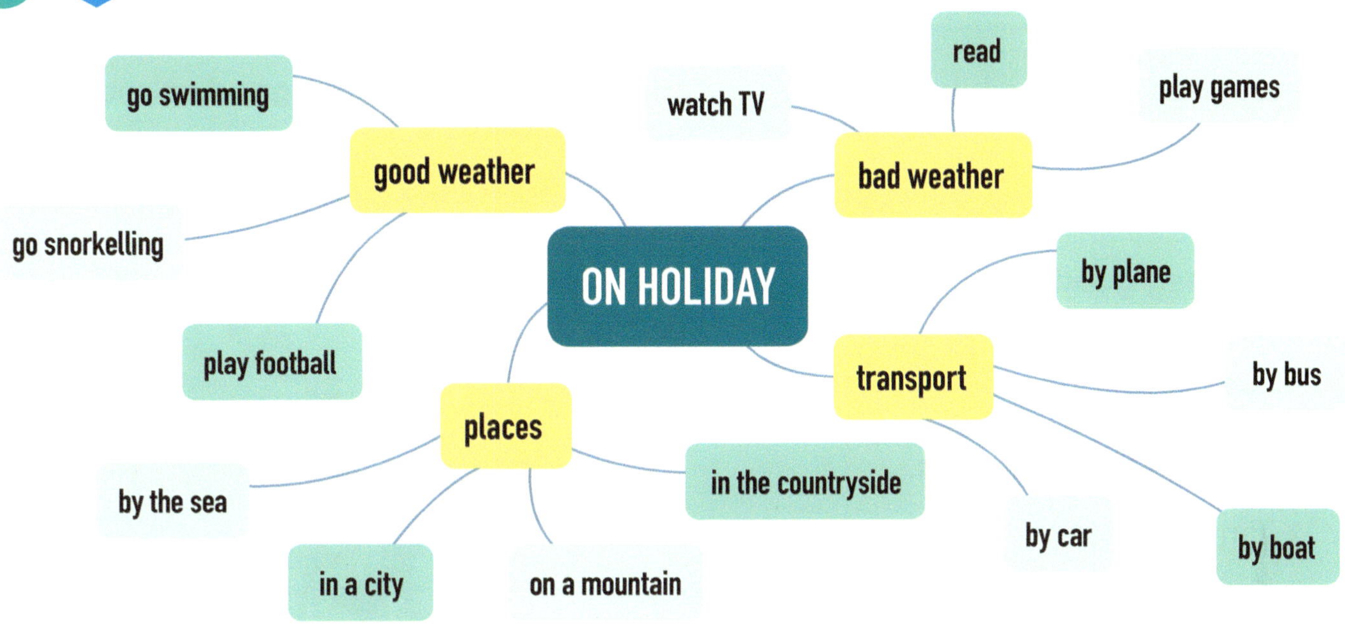

2 Close your eyes for a minute. Imagine you are on holiday now. Write your ideas.

- Where are you? (at home / in another country)
- What was the weather like the last few days? (sunny / rainy / ...)
- What did you do? (went snorkelling / read a book / ...)
- What are you going to do in the next few days? (play games / ...)

3 Write an email about your holiday.

Writing tip

Use 'Hi', Hello' or 'Dear' to start emails. Finish with 'See you soon', 'Love' or 'Best wishes'.

To: Anna@superminds.com
Subject: Hello from Wales!

Hello Anna,
We're on holiday in Wales. It's great. We're in a hotel by the sea. The last few days the weather wasn't good. It rained, but that wasn't a problem. We had lots of fun. We played games and read. In the evenings, we watched DVDs. The next few days are going to be better. We're going to swim in the sea and play football on the beach. On Sunday, we're going to go hiking.
Love,
Trish

Language focus Meet The Explorers

Be good at + ing

I**'m** not **good at** rid**ing** bikes.	He**'s**/She**'s**/It**'s** not very **good at** cook**ing**.
You**'re** not **good at** snorkell**ing**.	We**'re good at** climb**ing** trees.
He**'s**/She**'s**/It**'s good at** play**ing** football.	They**'re** not **good at** play**ing** tennis.
Are you/they **good at** danc**ing**?	Yes, I/we/they **am**/**are**.
Is he/she **good at** play**ing** the piano?	No, he/she **is**n't.

1 **Complete the sentences.**

1 I'm good at __________ a kite.
2 Our sister's not good at __________ horses.
3 My dad's not good at __________ breakfast.
4 They're good at __________ French.
5 We're not good at __________ puzzles.

Possessive apostrophe

Penny is Ben**'s** sister.	Paula**'s** dog is very friendly.
Vivian is Jack**'s** mum.	Dad**'s** car is very old.
Ian**'s** bike is red.	My uncle**'s** house is very big.

Paula's dog is very friendly.

2 **Circle the correct word.**

1 My **mum** / **mum's** is really nice.
2 My **mum** / **mum's** sister is my aunt.
3 **Brian** / **Brian's** bike is new.
4 **Brian** / **Brian's** is my friend.
5 I like **Sally** / **Sally's** cat.

1 Our school

Like / Don't like + ing

I/You **like** writ**ing** stories.
He/She **loves** play**ing** computer games.
The dog **doesn't like** eat**ing** vegetables.
We/They **love** go**ing** to the cinema.
We/They **don't like** learn**ing** Maths.

Do you/they **like** do**ing** homework? Yes, I/we/they do.
Does he/she **like** sing**ing** in class? No, he/she doesn't.

1 **Circle the correct word.**

1 Mike likes **play / playing** football.
2 I really don't like **walking / walk** to school.
3 They love **playing / play** computer games.
4 Do you like **cook / cooking**?

The dog doesn't like eating vegetables.

Have to / has to + infinitive

Do you/they **have to go** to school on Saturdays? No, I/we/they don't.
Does he/she **have to make** breakfast in the morning? Yes, he/she does.
I/You **have to do** homework every day.
Tom/Paula **has to wash** the dog every Sunday.
We/They **have to be** home before eight o'clock.

2 **Put the words in order.**

1 have / wear / uniform / I / to / school

______________________________.

2 your / to / eat / have / you / beans

______________________________.

3 John / today / has / school / to / to / walk

______________________________.

Paula has to wash the dog every Sunday.

2 The picnic

Questions and answers with *some* and *any*

Is there **any** salad?	Yes, there is **some** salad. / No, there isn't **any** salad.
Are there **any** grapes?	Yes, there are **some** grapes. / No, there aren't **any** grapes.

1 Write *some* or *any*.

1 There aren't __________ parks in our town.
2 Are there __________ biscuits in the cupboard?
3 There's __________ fish in this salad. Yuck!
4 There are __________ cats in the garden.
5 Is there __________ juice in the fridge?

Suggestions

Shall we **go** to the cinema? Good idea!
Shall we **dance**? No, thank you.
How about some sandwiches? OK.

2 Put the words in order.

1 soup / dinner / we / shall / have / for

______________________________?

2 some / about / lemonade / how

______________________________?

3 cheese / lunch / how / a / for / about / sandwich

______________________________?

3 Daily tasks

Telling the time

What time is it?

 It's eleven **o'clock**.

 It's **half past** eleven.

 It's **quarter past** eleven.

 It's **quarter to** twelve.

1 Look and complete the sentences.

1  It's __________ __________ two.

3  It's __________ __________ eleven.

2  It's __________ __________ seven.

4  It's __________ __________ four.

Adverbs for time

I **never** do homework on Saturdays.
He **sometimes** does the shopping.

We **usually** go to bed before eight o'clock.
They **always** say 'please' and 'thank you'.

Do you **always** get up at seven o'clock?

Yes, I **do**. / No, I **don't**.

2 Put the words in order.

1 mum / help / my / I / kitchen / always / the / in

____.

2 me / to / usually / Kevin / walks / school / with

____.

3 sometimes / dad / cooks / my / dinner

____.

He sometimes does the shopping.

4 Around town

Prepositions

The cat is above the TV.

My house is **opposite** the school.
The café's **near** the bank.
Where's your school?

The cat's **above** the TV.
My bag's **below** the stairs.
It's **near** the park.

1 Look and complete the sentences.

1 The sofa is __________ the painting.
2 The sofa is __________ the TV.
3 The clock is __________ the TV.
4 The baby is __________ the table.

Be going to + infinitive of purpose

Where are you/we/they going? I'**m**/We'**re**/They'**re going to** the shops **to get** some milk.
Where's he/she going? He'**s**/She'**s going to** the flower shop **to buy** some flowers.

I'**m**/You'**re**/We'**re**/They'**re going to** the pool **to go** swimming.
He'**s**/She'**s going to** the station **to take** a train.

2 Complete the sentences.

1 I'm going to the __________________ to play tennis.
2 She's going to the __________________ to get a book.
3 We're going to the __________________ to wait for a bus.
4 Dad's going to the __________________ to get some money.
5 They're going to the __________________ to see a film.

5 Under the sea

Was / Were

I **was** really tired last night.	It **was** quiet in the classroom.
You **were** very angry.	We **weren't** at school today.
He **was** my friend.	They **were** very happy to see us.
She **wasn't** very happy.	

1 **Write *was* or *were*.**

1 My grandfather __________ a teacher.
2 I __________ very sad.
3 My dad's first car __________ pink!
4 Yes, we __________ at the party.
5 Jim and Tony __________ scared of the octopus.

Questions and answers with *was / were*

Were you at school?	Yes, I **was**.	No, I **wasn't**.
Was he/she at home?	Yes, he/she **was**.	No, he/she **wasn't**.
Where **were** you?	I **was** at my aunt's house.	

2 **Circle the correct word.**

1 **Was / Were** the lesson difficult?
2 Where **was / were** the books?
3 **Was / Were** Nathan and Adam at the party?
4 Where **was / were** your mum's car keys?
5 **Was / Were** there a dolphin in the sea?

6 Gadgets

Comparatives

My car is **faster than** yours.
Your shoes are **cleaner than** my shoes.
The blue mobile phone is **more expensive than** the red one.
Maths is **more difficult than** Science.
Your ice cream is **bigger than** my ice cream!
I think Ben is **happier than** me today.

1 Use comparatives to complete the sentences.

1 Their car is __________ than our car. (expensive)
2 His scooter is __________ than my scooter. (big)
3 That garden is __________ than our garden. (beautiful)
4 My skateboard is __________ than your skateboard. (cheap)
5 Rachel is always __________ than her sister. (happy)

Superlatives

It's **the biggest** cat in the world.
He's **the happiest** person in my family.
This is **the cheapest** mobile phone in the shop.
The smallest park in the world is in the United States.
It's **the most exciting** film ever!

2 Put the words in order.

1 class / in / our / I'm / smallest / the / boy
______________________________.
2 beautiful / in / most / Africa / snake / the / it's
______________________________.
3 it's / on / the / beach / the / sandcastle / biggest
______________________________.
4 footballer / most / the / world's / expensive / he's
______________________________.

7 In the hospital

Past simple: regular verbs

I/You play**ed** basketball yesterday.
She/He walk**ed** to school this morning.
The helicopter land**ed** on the building.
We/They watch**ed** TV after school.

1 Use the verbs in brackets to talk about yesterday.

1 I ________ into the swimming pool. The water was very cold! (jump)
2 We ________ at his hat. (smile)
3 My sister ________ dinner last night. (cook)
4 My aunt ________ me with my homework yesterday. (help)
5 Ursula and Bridget ________ computer games in the afternoon. (play)

The helicopter landed on the building.

Past simple: irregular verbs

I **felt** tired all day.
You **rode** a dinosaur! Really?
Mr Linford **gave** me the wrong book.
She **went** to bed at eight o'clock.
It **said**, 'Miaow', I think.
We **had** a lot to eat at lunch.
They **woke up** at half past six.

2 Write the infinitives.

1 felt ________
2 gave ________
3 had ________
4 woke up ________
5 went ________
6 said ________

8 Around the world

Negatives with past simple

I **didn't play** hockey!
You **didn't eat** all your food.
He **didn't visit** his grandfather on Sunday.
She **didn't like** my present.
It **didn't snow** last night.
We **didn't go** to school today.
They **didn't want** to help me.

1 **Complete the sentences.**

1 They went to England, but they ________ to London.
2 She gave me a present, but she ________ one to my sister.
3 We had Maths today, but we ________ History.
4 I felt ill last night, but I ________ ill this morning.
5 He had some sandwiches, but he ________ any lemonade.

She didn't like my present.

Questions and answers with past simple

Did you **have** fun at the party?	Yes, I **did**.	
Did he/she **say**, 'Thank you'?	No, he **didn't**.	Yes, she **did**.
Did we/they **do** something wrong?	Yes, you **did**.	No, they **didn't**.
When **did** you **see** Aaron?	Yesterday.	
Where **did** you **see** him?	At school.	

2 **Complete the questions and answers.**

1 ________ you do the shopping? Yes, I ________.
2 ________ she find her cat? No, she ________.
3 ________ they go by train? No, they ________.
4 ________ we win? No, we ________.
5 ________ he help you? Yes, he ________.

9 Holiday plans

Future with *be going to* + infinitive

I'**m going to send** you a postcard.
You **aren't going to eat** that!
He'**s going to buy** a new raincoat.
She **isn't going to take** the bus today.
It'**s going to be** windy tomorrow.
We'**re going to play** tennis now.
They'**re going to learn** French.

1 Complete the sentences.

not rain | cook | build | phone | not have

1 I'm ______________ Lisa this evening.
2 It ______________ this afternoon.
3 You're ______________ dinner.
4 We ______________ fish and chips for dinner.
5 Dad's ______________ me a new tree house.

Questions and answers with *be going to* + infinitive

Am I **going to get** better soon?	Yes, you are.
Are you **going to watch** TV at the weekend?	Yes, I am.
Is he/she **going to make** a cake for your birthday?	Yes, he/she is.
Are we/they **going to take** the bus?	No, we/they aren't.

2 Use the verbs in brackets to talk about the future.

1 Are you __________ your grandparents this weekend? (visit)
2 Is he __________ at your house tonight? (sleep)
3 Are your mum and dad __________ you with your school project? (help)
4 Is your sister __________ you a birthday present? (give)
5 Are we __________ pizza tonight? (have)